Spiritual Assessment and Intervention with Older Adults: Current Directions and Applications

Spiritual Assessment and Intervention with Older Adults: Current Directions and Applications has been co-published simultaneously as *Journal of Religion, Spirituality & Aging,* Volume 17, Numbers 1/2 2004.

Monographic Separates from the *Journal of Religion, Spirituality & Aging*™

For additional information on these and other Haworth Press titles, including descriptions, tables of contents, reviews, and prices, use the QuickSearch catalog at http://www.HaworthPress.com.

The *Journal of Religion, Spirituality & Aging*™ is the successor title to *Journal of Religious Gerontology** Which changed title after Vol. 16, No. 3/4, 2004 and *Journal of Religion & Aging*, which changed title after Vol. 6, No. 3/4, 1989. The *Journal of Religion, Spirituality & Aging*™, under its new title, begins with Vol. 17, No. 1/2, 2004.

Spiritual Assessment and Intervention with Older Adults: Current Directions and Applications, edited by Mark Brennan, PhD, and Deborah Heiser, PhD (Vol. 17, No. 1/2, 2004). *OUTSTANDING. . . . Provides readers with the most up-to-date and authoritative perspectives on spiritual assessment and intervention in the field of aging. Editors Brennan and Heiser offer an introduction in which they deftly and concisely summarize current trends and practical applications in this sub-specialty. The chapters on elder abuse, Alzheimer's disease, and intergenerational programs are all rich with illustrations that will help clinicians develop new applications for reaching target populations. I was particularly impressed by Heiser, Brennan, and Redic's discussion of the 'CARE Cabinet' collection of intervention techniques. What the editors have done is to strike an exemplary balance between theory and practice. This is a book that will be helpful to many readers for years to come."* (Harry R. Moody, PhD, Director of Academic Affairs, AARP).

Practical Theology for Aging, edited by Rev. Derrel R. Watkins, PhD* (Vol. 15, No. 1/2, 2003). *"THOUGHT-PROVOKING, ENLIGHTENING, INSIGHTFUL, AND PRACTICAL. As I read through the book, I repeatedly found myself thinking, 'WHAT AN EXCELLENT SUPPLEMENTAL TEXT for the Introduction to Gerontology course.' AN EXCELLENT TRAINING RESOURCE for health care providers working with older adults, as well as religious leaders of all denominations as they seek to enhance their pastoral care programs with older adults."* (Patricia Gleason-Wynn, PhD, Lecturer, School of Social Work, Baylor University).

New Directions in the Study of Late Life Religiousness and Spirituality, edited by Susan H. McFadden, PhD, Mark Brennan, PhD, and Julie Hicks Patrick, PhD* (Vol. 14, No. 1, 2/3, 2003). *"Refreshing. . . . encouraging. . . . This book has given us a gift of evolving thoughts and perspectives on religion and spirituality in the later years of life. . . . Of interest not only to university students, researchers, and scholars, but also to those who provide services to the aged."* (James Birren, PhD, Associate Director, UCLA Center on Aging).

Aging Spirituality and Pastoral Care: A Multi-National Perspective, edited by Rev. Elizabeth MacKinlay, RN, PhD, Rev. James W. Ellor, PhD, DMin, DCSW, and Rev. Stephen Pickard, PhD* (Vol. 12, No. 3/4, 2001). *"Comprehensive . . . The authors are not just thinkers and scholars. They speak from decades of practical expertise with the aged, demented, and dying."* (Bishop Tom Frame, PhD, Lecturer in Public Theology, St. Mark's National Theological Centre, Canberra, Australia)

Religion and Aging: An Anthology of the Poppele Papers, edited by Derrel R. Watkins, PhD, MSW, MRE* (Vol. 12, No. 2, 2001). *"Within these pages, the new ministry leader is supplied with the core prerequisites for effective older adult ministry and the more experienced leader is provided with an opportunity to reconnect with timeless foundational principles. Insights into the interior of the aging experience, field-tested and proven techniques and ministry principles, theological rationale for adult care giving, Biblical perspectives on aging, and philosophic and spiritual insights into the aging process."* (Dennis R. Myers, LMSW-ACP, Director, Baccalaureate Studies in Social Work, Baylor University, Waco, Texas)

Aging in Chinese Society: A Holistic Approach to the Experience of Aging in Taiwan and Singapore, edited by Homer Jernigan and Margaret Jernigan* (Vol. 8, No. 3, 1992). *"A vivid introduction to aging in these societies. . . . Case studies illustrate the interaction of religion, personality, immigration, modernization, and aging."* (Clinical Gerontologist)

Spiritual Maturity in the Later Years, edited by James J. Seeber* (Vol. 7, No. 1/2, 1991). *"An excellent introduction to the burgeoning field of gerontology and religion."* (Southwestern Journal of Theology)

Gerontology in Theological Education: Local Program Development, edited by Barbara Payne and Earl D. C. Brewer** (Vol. 6, No. 3/4, 1989). *"Directly relevant to gerontological education in other contexts and to applications in the educational programs and other work of church congregations and community agencies for the aging." (The Newsletter of the Christian Sociological Society)*

Gerontology in Theological Education, edited by Barbara Payne and Earl D. C. Brewer** (Vol. 6, No. 1/2, 1989). *"An excellent resource for seminaries and anyone interested in the role of the church in the lives of older persons . . . must for all libraries." (David Maldonado, DSW, Associate Professor of Church & Society, Southern Methodist University, Perkins School of Theology)*

Religion, Aging and Health: A Global Perspective, compiled by the World Health Organization, edited by William M. Clements** (Vol. 4, No. 3/4, 1989). *"Fills a long-standing gap in gerontological literature. This book presents an overview of the interrelationship of religion, aging, and health from the perspective of the world's major faith traditions that is not available elsewhere . . . " (Stephen Sapp, PhD, Associate Professor of Religious Studies, University of Miami, Coral Gables, Florida)*

New Directions in Religion and Aging, edited by David B. Oliver** (Vol. 3, No. 1/2, 1987). *"This book is a telescope enabling us to see the future. The data of the present provides a solid foundation for seeing the future." (Dr. Nathan Kollar, Professor of Religious Studies and Founding Chair, Department of Gerontology, St. John Fisher College; Adjunct Professor of Ministerial Theology, St. Bernard's Institute)*

The Role of the Church in Aging, Volume 3: Programs and Services for Seniors, edited by Michael C. Hendrickson** (Vol. 2, No. 4, 1987). *Experts explore an array of successful programs for the elderly that have been implemented throughout the United States in order to meet the social, emotional, religious, and health needs of the elderly.*

The Role of the Church in Aging, Volume 2: Implications for Practice and Service, edited by Michael C. Hendrickson** (Vol. 2, No. 3, 1986). *Filled with important insight and state-of-the-art concepts that reflect the cutting edge of thinking among religion and aging professionals. (Rev. James W. Ellor, DMin, AM, CSW, ACSW, Associate Professor, Department Chair, Human Service Department, National College of Education, Lombard, Illinois)*

The Role of the Church in Aging, Volume 1: Implications for Policy and Action, edited by Michael C. Hendrickson** (Vol. 2, No. 1/2, 1986). *Reviews the current status of the religious sector's involvement in the field of aging and identifies a series of strategic responses for future policy and action.*

Published by

The Haworth Pastoral Press, 10 Alice Street, Binghamton, NY 13904-1580 USA

The Haworth Pastoral Press is an imprint of The Haworth Press, Inc., 10 Alice Street, Binghamton, NY 13904-1580 USA.

Spiritual Assessment and Intervention with Older Adults: Current Directions and Applications has been co-published simultaneously as *Journal of Religion, Spirituality & Aging*, Volume 17, Numbers 1/2 2004.

Cover design by Marylouise E. Doyle

Library of Congress Cataloging-in-Publication Data

Spiritual assessment and intervention with older adults: current directions and applications /Mark Brennan and Deborah Heiser, editors.
    p. cm.
    "Co-published simultaneously as Journal of religion, spirituality & aging, Volume 17, Numbers 1/2, 2004-T.p. verso.
    Includes bibliographical references and index.
    ISBN-13: 978-0-7890-2747-4 (hc. : alk. paper)
    ISBN-10: 0-7890-2747-X (hc. : alk. paper)
    ISBN-13: 978-0-7890-2748-1 (pbk. : alk. paper)
    ISBN-10: 0-7890-2748-8 (pbk. : alk. paper)
    1. Older people-Religious life. 2. Older people-Pastoral counseling of. I. Brennan, Mark (Mark G.) II. Heiser, Deborah.
BL625.4.S64 2004
259'.3-dc22
                                              2004020726

Spiritual Assessment and Intervention with Older Adults: Current Directions and Applications

Mark Brennan, PhD
Deborah Heiser, PhD
Editors

Spiritual Assessment and Intervention with Older Adults: Current Directions and Applications has been co-published simultaneously as *Journal of Religion, Spirituality & Aging*, Volume 17, Numbers 1/2 2004.

The Haworth Pastoral Press®
An Imprint of The Haworth Press, Inc.

New York • London • Victoria (AU)
www.HaworthPress.com

Indexing, Abstracting & Website/Internet Coverage

This section provides you with a list of major indexing & abstracting services and other tools for bibliographic access. That is to say, each service began covering this periodical during the year noted in the right column. Most Websites which are listed below have indicated that they will either post, disseminate, compile, archive, cite or alert their own Website users with research-based content from this work. (This list is as current as the copyright date of this publication.)

Abstracting, Website/Indexing Coverage . . . . Year When Coverage Began

- *Abstracts in Social Gerontology: Current Literature on Aging* **1991**
- *AgeInfo CD-Rom <http://www.cpa.org.uk>* **1995**
- *AgeLine Database <http://research.aarp.org/ageline>* **1990**
- *Applied Social Sciences Index & Abstracts (ASSIA)*
    (Online: ASSI via Data-Star) (CD-Rom: ASSIA Plus)
    <http://www.csa.com> **1994**
- *ATLA Religion Database with ATLASerials. This periodical*
    is indexed in ATLA Religion Database with ATLASerials,
    published by the American Theological Library Association
    <http://www.atla.com> **1991**
- *AURSI African Urban & Religion Science Index. A scholarly*
    and research index which synthesizes and compiles all publications
    on urbanization and regional science in Africa within the world.
    Published annually. **2004**
- *Christian Periodical Index <http://www.aci.org/cpi.htm>* . . . . *
- *EBSCOhost Electronic Journals Service (EJS)*
    <http://ejournals.ebsco.com> **2000**
- *Educational Administration Abstracts (EAA)* **1995**
- *Family & Society Studies Worldwide*
    <http://www.nisc.com> **1996**
- *Family Index Database <http://www.familyscholar.com>* **1995**

(continued)

* **Exact start date to come.**

Special Bibliographic Notes related to special journal issues
(separates) and indexing/abstracting:

- indexing/abstracting services in this list will also cover material in any "separate" that is co-published simultaneously with Haworth's special thematic journal issue or DocuSerial. Indexing/abstracting usually covers material at the article/chapter level.
- monographic co-editions are intended for either non-subscribers or libraries which intend to purchase a second copy for their circulating collections.
- monographic co-editions are reported to all jobbers/wholesalers/approval plans. The source journal is listed as the "series" to assist the prevention of duplicate purchasing in the same manner utilized for books-in-series.
- to facilitate user/access services all indexing/abstracting services are encouraged to utilize the co-indexing entry note indicated at the bottom of the first page of each article/chapter/contribution.
- this is intended to assist a library user of any reference tool (whether print, electronic, online, or CD-ROM) to locate the monographic version if the library has purchased this version but not a subscription to the source journal.
- individual articles/chapters in any Haworth publication are also available through the Haworth Document Delivery Service (HDDS).

Spiritual Assessment and Intervention with Older Adults: Current Directions and Applications

CONTENTS

ABOUT THE EDITORS

Mark Brennan, PhD, is Senior Research Associate at the Arlene R. Gordon Research Institute of Lighthouse International in New York City. Since 1997, he has conducted research on the effects of religiousness and spirituality in adapting to vision impairment among middle-age and older adults. Other work in this area included the "Postcards to God" study, in which adolescent and adult workshop participants created picture and text message postcards as a form of spiritual expression. Dr. Brennan's work in spirituality and religiousness has been published in *Journal of Religious Gerontology; International Journal of Psychology and Religion;* and *Journal of Adult Development*, and has been presented at a number of national and international conferences. He was also a co-editor of the Haworth Pastoral Press Publication *New Directions in the Study of Late Life Religiousness and Spirituality.* Other professional interests include lifespan personality development, informal and formal social supports, and minority aging issues.

He is a member of the Gerontological Society of America, the American Psychological Association (Division 36-Psychology of Religion; Division 20-Adult Development and Aging), and the State Society on Aging of New York. In 1993, he was awarded a fellowship from the Hunter-Brookdale Center on Aging in recognition of contributions to the study of older New Yorkers. He was also named a New York State Scholar for Project 2015 by the State Office of Aging, and is a recent recipient of the Pride Senior Network Recognition Award for research on the older gay, lesbian, transgender and bisexual population.

Other publications of Dr. Brennan's work have appeared in *The Gerontologist;* the *Journal of Gerontological Social Work; Qualitative Social Work: Research and Practice; Perceptual and Motor Skills;* The *Journal of Social Work in Disability & Rehabilitation;* and *Journal of General Psychology.* In 2000, he co-authored *Social Care of the Elderly: The Effects of Ethnicity, Class and Culture.* Other work has appeared in *The Lighthouse Handbook of Vision Impairment and Vision Rehabilitation,* and *Lifespan Development and Behavior Vol. 11.*

Deborah Heiser, PhD, is Researcher at Isabella Geriatric Center in New York City. She received her PhD in Applied Developmental Psychology from Fordham University in 2002. Since that time, Dr. Heiser has conducted research on depression, palliative care, and spirituality in the long-term care setting. Her work in these areas has been presented at national and international conferences. She has also published in *Clinical Gerontologist.*

She is a member of the Gerontological Society of America, the American Psychological Association, the State Society on Aging of New York (board member), Psychologists in Long-Term Care, Sigma Xi, Eastern Psychological Association, and the Society for the Exploration of Psychotherapy Integration. In 2003, she was awarded the National Student Research Award given by Psychologists in Long-Term Care in recognition of post-doctoral research focused on depression identification and treatment in the long-term care setting.

Introduction:
Spiritual Assessment
and Intervention:
Current Directions
and Applications

Mark Brennan, PhD
Deborah Heiser, PhD

SUMMARY. There is a growing literature documenting the positive effects of religiousness and spirituality. As a result, the assessment of spirituality, and interventions that tap into this personal resource, are becoming increasingly the focus of research and practice in many populations, including older adults. Spiritual assessment may include a variety of modalities that obtain information about a person's spiritual well-being, history, crises or dilemmas. Such assessments are used to guide pastoral care and/or interventions. Any programs, policy, procedure, or protocol that address the spiritual well-being and needs of individuals can be considered a spiritual intervention. These interventions

---

Mark Brennan is Senior Research Associate, Lighthouse International, 111 East 59th Street, New York, NY 10022 (E-mail: mbrennan@lighthouse.org). Deborah Heiser is Research Associate, Isabella Geriatric Center, 515 Audubon Avenue, New York, NY 10040 (E-mail: dheiser@isabella.org).

[Haworth co-indexing entry note]: "Introduction: Spiritual Assessment and Intervention: Current Directions and Applications." Brennan, Mark, and Deborah Heiser. Co-published simultaneously in *Journal of Religion, Spirituality & Aging* (The Haworth Pastoral Press, an imprint of The Haworth Press, Inc.) Vol. 17, No. 1/2, 2004, pp. 1-20; and: *Spiritual Assessment and Intervention with Older Adults: Current Directions and Applications* (ed: Mark Brennan, and Deborah Heiser) The Haworth Pastoral Press, an imprint of The Haworth Press, Inc., 2004, pp. 1-20. Single or multiple copies of this article are available for a fee from The Haworth Document Delivery Service [1-800-HAWORTH, 9:00 a.m. - 5:00 p.m. (EST). E-mail address: docdelivery@haworthpress.com].

may consist of activities that strengthen, reinforce or promote the spiritual and religious resources of individuals, or that utilize existing spiritual resources present in the individual to address well-being and needs regarding spirituality and other life domains. It is imperative that as this work moves forward, spiritual assessment and intervention be firmly grounded both conceptually and empirically, and that high standards of scientific rigor are maintained in research and application. Without such attention to detail, both basic and applied research may lack the credibility to make a strong case for meeting the needs of older adults through spiritual assessment and intervention. *[Article copies available for a fee from The Haworth Document Delivery Service: 1-800-HAWORTH. E-mail address: <docdelivery@haworthpress.com> Website: <http://www.HaworthPress.com> © 2004 by The Haworth Press, Inc. All rights reserved.]*

KEYWORDS. Assessment, intervention, religiousness, spirituality, older adults

There is a growing literature documenting the positive effects religiousness and spirituality have as buffers to life stress, such as chronic or terminal illness (Saunders, 1988), caregiver burden (Picot, Debanne, Namazi, & Wykle, 1997), mental illness (Lindgren & Coursey, 1995), substance abuse (Brizer, 1993), and social disruption resulting from war (Pargament et al., 1994). Generally, results from these studies show that greater levels of religiousness and spirituality lead to improved physical and mental health outcomes (Pargament, 1997). Although the topic of spirituality is not restricted to older people, the papers presented in this volume focus on this population.

Pargament (1997) notes that one major function of religious beliefs is that they promote positive appraisals of negative situations. For example, a caregiver of a parent with Alzheimer's Disease can consider that situation as leading to personal and spiritual growth. Despite some methodological concerns with empirical findings (Sloan, Bagiella, & Powell, 1999), spirituality and religiousness have been found to exert positive effects on physical and mental health, coping, and adjustment in a wide variety of populations, including older adults. As a result, spirituality is being addressed and discussed by nursing, medicine, mental health, and business organizations (Patton, 2001). It is also becoming increasingly the focus of research and practice, some of which is reviewed in this issue. In order to provide some context for the reader, we begin by defining our terms of spirituality, religiousness, assessment, and intervention.

WHAT IS SPIRITUAL ASSESSMENT AND INTERVENTION?

As attention to the areas of spirituality and religiousness in the social and health sciences has blossomed in the past decades, so too have concerns on how we define, measure and operationalize these concepts in research and practice (McFadden, Brennan, & Patrick, 2003a, 2003b). In the main, most would agree that religiousness and spirituality are inter-related, yet distinct (Hill & Pargament, 2003; Miller & Thoresen, 2003; Moberg, 2002; Pargament, 1997). Beyond this point of agreement, most of the debate centers on how these constructs relate to each other, the degree to which they overlap, and how best to operationalize them (McFadden et al., 2003a, 2003b; Miller & Thoresen, 2003).

McDonald (2000) posits that spirituality is an additional and orthogonal personality trait in comparison to other traits assessed in traditional models (e.g., neuroticism, extraversion, openness to experience). Spirituality has many personality trait-like qualities, being relatively stable within-individuals over time, and demonstrating high degrees of variability (i.e., individual differences) in a variety of populations. Adopting this perspective, we consider spirituality in its broadest sense, that is, as a predilection toward metaphysical concerns. Well-recognized components of spirituality include a sense of transcendence, inner-integration, connectedness to others, and purpose and meaning in life (Chandler, Holden, & Kolander, 1992; Hawks, 1994; Howden, 1992; Lindgren & Coursey, 1995; Moberg, 1967; Pargament, 1997; Saunders, 1988; Seeward, 1992). Furthermore, there is a growing body of empirical work that shows differential effects of spirituality and religiousness when these constructs are considered individually, with most, albeit limited, findings to date, pointing to spirituality rather than religious practice per se as the source of the positive effects of religiousness on psychosocial outcomes (Brennan, 2004; Fry, 2000, 2001; Nelson, Rosenfeld, Breitbart, & Galietta, 2002). For example, Daaleman, Subashan, and Studenski (2004) conducted a study to assess the effects of religion and spirituality on self-reported health status of older adults. Participants who reported greater spirituality but not religiosity were more likely to state that they were in good health. Daaleman and colleagues thus concluded that spirituality was an important correlate of positive subjective health status in older adults.

However, it is important to recognize that for most individuals spirituality *is* expressed through religiousness (Hill & Pargament, 2003; Pargament, 1997), namely, adherence to a set of ideological beliefs, rituals, and practices associated with particular creeds, denominations or sects (Lindgren & Coursey, 1995; Moberg, 1967). Thus, while religiousness is typically the outward manifestation of the inner spiritual life, spirituality can exist in the absence of religious affiliation, whereas religiousness in and of itself does not guarantee a developed spirituality (Allport & Ross, 1967; Chandler et al., 1992; Moberg, 1967; Ross, 1990).

Spiritual Assessment

Spiritual Assessment may include a variety of modalities, both formal and informal, that obtain information about a person's spiritual well-being, history, crises or dilemmas. The results of such an assessment are typically used to guide pastoral care and/or interventions. For example, a life review that has a spiritual emphasis may serve as one form of a spiritual assessment (LeFavi & Wessels, 2003). One goal of such assessments is to better understand how spiritual issues affect the individual and significant others and whether or not spiritual beliefs may be enlisted as an additional personal resource for dealing with the issue at hand (Moncher & Josephson, 2004).

Spiritual assessment also allows providers to better accommodate the beliefs of the patient or consumer, and has even been incorporated as part of medical school training (King, Blue, Mallin, & Thiedke, 2004). Traditionally, the Western perspective has not taken a holistic approach to addressing physical and psychological health by considering community-based formal health and social care to be separate domains from spirituality. For example, the World Health Organization (1948) in its definition of health does not include spiritual well-being. This is in contrast to Eastern approaches to health that consider spirituality an important constituent of a model of care that integrates body, mind and spirit (Chan, Ho, & Chow, 2001).

However, attitudes toward the inclusion of spirituality in applied settings are changing. For example, the Joint Commission on Accreditation of Healthcare Organizations (JCAHO) requires spiritual assessments for hospitals, long-term care facilities, and home care. These spiritual assessments are intended to gauge the impact of spirituality on care being provided to clients. Example questions of what JCAHO (2004) suggest should be in a spiritual assessment include:

- Who or what provides the patient with strength and hope?
- Does the patient use prayer in his or her life?
- How does the patient express his or her spirituality?
- What does suffering mean to the patient?
- What does dying mean to the patient?
- How does the patient keep going day after day?

But spirituality and religiousness are multidimensional constructs that defy easy definitions and quantitative assessment (Anandarajah & Hight, 2001; Chatters & Taylor, 1998; Ellison, 1998; McCullough, Hoyt, Larson, Koenig, & Thoresen, 2000; Peidmont, 2001; Sloan, Bagiella, & Powell, 1999). For example, Howden's (1992) Spirituality Assessment Scale contains four dimensions including transcendence, purpose and meaning in life, reliance on inner resources, and a sense of interconnectedness with others. Although there are a number of similar measures that incorporate such a multidimensional framework (e.g., Fetzer Institute/NIA Working Group, 1999), there are limits to the quantitative measurement approach (Hodge, 2001; Nosek & Hughes, 2001).

The potential to engage in spiritual interventions is constrained by our ability to conduct accurate, reliable and meaningful spiritual assessments. Some of the difficulties in applying a standardized approach to assessing spirituality include the idiosyncratic and personal nature of spirituality, difficulty and reluctance in employing scientific means to examining profound spiritual and existential issues, and the utilization of standardized assessment approaches to multicultural and multireligious populations in a way that does not bias the assessment (Mokuau, Hishinuma, & Nishimura, 2001).

In addressing the incompatibility of quantitative measures for the assessment of spirituality Hodge (2001) notes, ". . . quantitative instruments presuppose a certain construction of reality and in the process leave little room for clients to negotiate a shared understanding of their individual experience with workers. The subjective, often intangible, nature of human existence is not captured" (p. 204). Hodge further states that quantitative approaches fail to address the realities of disparate spiritual traditions, and argues that spiritual assessment is best served with qualitative approaches. For example, many quantitative measures require modifications for use with non-Christian participants (e.g., Brennan, 2004). However, qualitative assessments of spirituality are presently limited in number, consisting mainly of religious/spiritual histories, open-ended interviews, and sentence completion techniques. However, one method utilizes pictorial representations in an autobiographical approach toward "significant events and experiences" (Hodge, 2001).

Spiritual Intervention

Any programs, policy, procedure, or protocol that address the spiritual well-being and needs of individuals can be considered a spiritual intervention. Such interventions may consist of activities that strengthen, reinforce or promote the spiritual and religious resources of individuals, or that utilize existing spiritual resources present in the individual (e.g., connections with a religious congregation, meditation practices) to address well-being and needs regarding spirituality and other life domains (e.g., health). For example in medical environments, spiritual assessment and intervention are used regularly in a variety of circumstances, such as prior to surgery, when a patient receives difficult news, when the patient appears sad, hopeless, frightened, discouraged, or when requested (Hover, 2004). Leder (1999-2000) notes that presently there are few programs designed to address the spiritual well-being of community-dwelling older adults.

Crowther, Parker, Achenbaum, Larimore, and Koenig (2002) have argued that spiritual well-being is an overlooked constituent of Rowe and Kahn's (1998) model of successful aging and, as such, should be the focus of active intervention to promote quality-of-life in the older population. Given the well-documented connections between spirituality and life quality for persons facing challenging life situations or for those with serious illness (e.g., Brennan, 2004; Fry 2000; 2001; Saunders, 1988), spiritual well-being is increasingly acknowledged as a valid target for intervention in these populations (Brady, Peterman, Fitchett, Mo, & Cella, 1999; Marcus, Elkins, & Mott, 2003; McClain, Rosenfeld, & Breitbart, 2003; Westlake & Dracup, 2001). Although a review of the literature on spiritual intervention is presented below, it should also be stressed that spiritual assessment may be, in itself, a form of intervention (LeFavi & Wessels, 2003). That is, providing patients and consumers the opportunity to articulate spiritual issues and concerns is supportive of spiritual well-being and may have therapeutic effects.

ISSUES IN THE APPLICATION OF SPIRITUAL ASSESSMENT AND INTERVENTION

Miller and Thoresen (2003) describe how, despite the large body of work on spiritual and religious processes, these domains rarely emerge in the training of health practitioners and social scientists. This has contributed to what these authors describe as two limiting assumptions: that spirituality *should not* and *cannot* be studied scientifically. However, despite the numinous nature of these constructs, there is little compelling evidence that these assumptions are valid or that methodological limitations in measuring these unobserved constructs are more problematic than other areas of inquiry in the social sciences (Miller & Thoresen, 2003).

It should also be noted that there is a concern on the part of many providers and scientists that inclusion of spiritual and religious domains in their work will promote political and cultural agendas that are at odds with their own values, as well as those of clients, consumers, and research participants (Brooks & Koenig, 2002). That is, there is a pervasive misperception that spiritual, and especially religious, values are necessarily conservative and fundamentalist, and therefore at odds with the traditionally positivistic, humanist and secular basis of social sciences and human services. However, this ignores the fact that progressive social values and religious/spiritual concerns are not mutually exclusive. It does explain the resistance to research on the effects of spirituality and religiousness in applied settings. That is, such work often meets with stiff resistance because the implications of positive results would suggest that spiritual assessment and intervention should be included in the provision of services.

Idiosyncratic Nature of Religious and Spiritual Beliefs

Spiritual assessments are designed to help identify individuals who need assistance in the expression of spirituality or who are having issues related to spiritual well-being. Spiritual assessments and interventions are not used to impose values, beliefs, or practices on another. Rather, spirituality is very personal, and may or may not be connected with religious expression. Furthermore, even within a particular faith tradition, there may be a great deal of variability. For example, the rituals, practices and discipline of Orthodox Jews are markedly different from Reform Jews. Even amongst Orthodox Jews, sharp differences exist between Hassidim and other sects. But such divergence does not end at the level of denomination or sect. Religious and spiritual beliefs can be very idiosyncratic, even within the parameters of a specialized faith tradition. Take, for example, a person who narrowly escapes death at a young age who develops a belief that she was spared in order to perform a special "mission" for her Higher Power. Thus, the very personal nature of religious and spiritual belief makes sensitivity to clients and consumers paramount.

In addition to the varieties of spiritual belief and expression, it should be emphasized that many individuals hold these as core values that define their very personhood (Allport & Ross, 1967). Thus, it is essential that providers respect the beliefs of clients and consumers. A "one-size-fits-all" approach to spiritual assessment and intervention is clearly inadvisable. Additionally, the intensely personal nature of this subject and the power dynamics of the provider-consumer relationship give rise to potential abuses and misapplications. Such "spiritual abuse" may take many forms, from proselytization and coercion, to the imposition of the provider's beliefs on the client and her situation (Miller & Thoresen, 2003). As Brooks and Koenig (2002) note, many of these potential pitfalls can be avoided through careful program planning and implementation.

There are also important considerations in the implementation of any intervention, including those designed to address spirituality. It should be emphasized that some form of spiritual assessment should be conducted prior to the implementation of any spiritual intervention in order to address the specific spiritual needs and issues of the individual. As noted above, religious and spiritual beliefs vary widely, and one cannot assume that individuals in the same situation necessarily have the same needs (e.g., end-of-life care). Kub, Nolan, Hughes et al. (2003) note that spiritual assessment in hospital settings are typically limited to asking patients about their religious affiliation or denomination. Such a limited approach does not begin to address the potential spiritual needs of patients. More detailed assessments are needed in order to adequately address the spiritual needs of hospital patients and other older adults who for various reasons are in need of spiritual support.

Finally, it is important that the efficacy of the intervention be assessed to determine effectiveness in terms of nurturing spiritual well-being and life quality. Incorporating some form of program evaluation is critical in order to insure that the intervention is being implemented as planned, and to demonstrate that it provides the expected and desired therapeutic effects. This may be easier in some settings than in others. For example, it would be relatively easy to obtain pre- and post-intervention measures of spiritual well-being among community-dwelling older adults enrolled in some type of leisure or recreational program in comparison to older adults who are frail, suffer from dementia, or are receiving palliative or hospice care.

EMPIRICAL FINDINGS ON SPIRITUAL INTERVENTION

Although there is a sizeable body of research that has focused on spiritual and religious effects on physical and mental health status, most of this work has not involved planned interventions. For example, Powell, Shahabi, and Thoresen (2003) provided an extensive review of studies on the relationship between spirituality, religion, and health, but most of these studies involved protective or passive effects of these factors. In the small group of studies that involved an active type of intervention, namely, praying for the recovery of sick individuals, the only demonstrable effects were on subjective indicators of questionable reliability. Similarly, Seeman, Fagan, Dublin, and Seeman (2003) reviewed the link between spiritual intervention, in the form of meditation, and underlying physiological processes (e.g., blood pressure) that could explain the generally positive research findings between religion, spirituality and health. While acknowledging an empirically based positive relation between such factors and basic physiological function, the authors concluded that more rigorous work in the field was needed.

Spiritual Interventions for Physical Health

In one of the few studies in the literature that addressed spiritual interventions to improve physical health, Gerard and colleagues examined the effects of participation in a spiritual-healing clinic using a randomized controlled trial (Gerard, Smith, & Simpson, 2003). Participants ($n = 68$) were adults 18 years or older with restricted neck movement and who were not receiving any form of spiritual healing at the start of the study. Participants were randomly assigned to spiritual intervention and control groups. The spiritual intervention consisted of 30-minute sessions with a spiritual healer three times per week; the control group received standard medical care. Following the intervention the treatment group scored significantly better than controls on neck rotation and flexion extension, pain severity, physical function, and energy/vitality, but significant between-group differences in levels of depression and chronic pain did not emerge. Although the authors note that these results do support the efficacy of spiritual intervention for physical ailments, they also note that larger studies of longer duration are needed to replicate these initial findings.

Spiritual Interventions for Mental Health and Psychological Well-Being

The work in the area of religious/spiritual interventions and psychosocial and mental health outcomes is also limited. Additionally, intervention programs conducted by, or in partnership with, faith-based organizations have rarely been formally evaluated in order to assess the practice and outcome differences between faith-based and secular providers (Binstock, 2002). In one study, Seeward (1992) described a program to improve spiritual well-being as the cornerstone of a larger wellness program aimed at the physical, emotional, mental, and *spiritual* components of well-being. The intervention consisted of two modalities: A seminar series and a journal-writing workshop. The seminar series presented a number of topics related to spiritual well-being, for example, codependency or creativity and humor. The journal-writing workshop was designed to provide participants with a space for self-reflection and inner exploration. Program evaluation revealed that attendance at the intervention was high and that participants reacted favorably to the experience. In addition, many participants reported making behavioral changes based on the content of these spiritual interventions.

In a second study that used an intervention to promote psychological well-being, 72 cardiac patients and spouses attended a retreat to promote positive changes in spirituality aimed at increasing general psychological well-being (Kennedy, Abbott, & Rosenberg, 2002). The intervention consisted of a two and one-half day retreat that included programs on healthy life-style options, stress management, communication, as well as spiritual principles of healing. Spiritual practice was also included in the intervention consisting of opportunities for prayer, meditation, yoga, and using visualization techniques. According to Kennedy and colleagues, nearly four in five participants reported increased spirituality following the retreat, and these spiritual changes were associated with improved psychological well-being on a number of indicators. These authors recommend the expansion of spiritual interventions in health care settings in order to address the spiritual and psychological well-being in these populations.

Although not the primary target of intervention, spirituality has been an essential component of twelve-step programs for persons with substance abuse issues or other socially undesirable behaviors (e.g., gambling). The first "step" in many of these programs, such as Alcoholics Anonymous, is the acknowledgement of a "Higher Power." To illustrate, Nealon-Woods and colleagues (1995) examined the relative importance of spiritual and social support factors in maintaining sobriety among male residents of a community residence for substance abusers. The authors downplayed the spiritual aspects since the majority of respondents reported that their "sense of fellowship" was responsible for regular attendance at meetings and maintaining sobriety. However, such vital connections with others have been recognized as a core component of spirituality (Chandler et al., 1992; Faull, Hills, & Cochrane et al., 2004; Howden, 1992; Lindgren & Coursey, 1995).

Other forms of spiritual intervention may utilize pre-existing connections to religious communities in order to address issues of physical and psychological well-being. Yanek and colleagues describe a program to improve cardiovascular health risks among middle-age and older African American women (n = 529) based in sixteen churches (Yanek, Becker, Moy, Gittelsohn, & Koffman, 2001). Standard behavioral and self-help interventions were compared to a behavioral intervention that contained a spiritual component. All three forms of the intervention targeted nutrition and physical activity levels that would lead to reduced risk of cardiovascular disease. One of the initial findings was that the standard behavioral intervention group spontaneously incorporated spiritual strategies. Thus, both the "standard" group and the "spiritual" group exhibited significant positive changes in body weight, waist circumference, dietary energy, blood pressure and sodium intake in comparison to the self-help group. The authors concluded that congregation-based interventions can be an important avenue to promote better cardiovascular health in this population.

Promoting the Intervention

As noted by Seeward (1992), there are numerous considerations when marketing interventions of a religious or spiritual nature to potential clients or consumers. Some individuals are put off by anything that has religious or spiritual overtones. Additionally, some individuals may not be forthcoming with issues related to their spiritual well-being, for example, living with devastating guilt, having negative emotions associated with spirituality (e.g., anger toward a spiritual leader), or being estranged from their religious community (e.g., "exiled" from a religious community or loss of trust in religious organizations; LaPierre,

2002). However, many people welcome the opportunity to address spiritual issues and have a desire to be involved in spiritually nurturing activities when facing serious health or life crises (Arnold, Avants, Margolin, & Marcotte, 2002; Kennedy, Abbott, & Rosenberg, 2002). Additionally, researchers have found that many people will spontaneously activate spiritual resources when facing life challenges, and would thus likely welcome the opportunity to participate in a spiritual intervention (Ai & Bolling, 2002; Dunn & Horgas, 2000; Yanek et al., 2001).

Seeward (1992) emphasized that the promotion of spiritual interventions must be sensitive to the context and population served. Thus, while "spiritual" may be perfectly appropriate in some circumstances, more neutral terms such as "transcendence" or "self-reliance" may work better in others. It is also crucial that those performing these interventions be well-trained and competent with the subject matter and materials so as not to threaten the integrity of the program and program leader (Seeward, 1992). In addition, adequate training of staff in handling issues related to spirituality is vital so that they are comfortable and confident in addressing this topic with patients and consumers (King, Blue, Mallin, & Thiedke, 2004; Wesley, Tunney, & Duncan, 2004).

OVERVIEW OF THE CONTENTS OF THIS VOLUME

The preceding introduction has addressed many of the major issues in current efforts at spiritual assessment and intervention in a variety of settings. This provides a context for understanding the contribution of the series of articles included in this volume. Five of the seven articles that follow were part of a symposium on spiritual assessment and intervention presented at the 2003 annual scientific meeting of the Gerontological Society of America in San Diego, California. All of the empirical papers in this volume are reporting on relatively recent work, and thus represent cutting-edge endeavors in the application of spiritual assessment and intervention. Furthermore, these articles represent the broad range of efforts on this topic, from conceptual concerns in the spiritual assessment process, to intervention needs-assessment and planning, the implementation of innovative intervention protocols, and the extension of proven interventions to new settings. Intervention settings range from faith-based congregations, to community-dwelling older adults and elderly in institutional settings. It is also noteworthy that the intervention research in this volume addresses some of the major challenges in the field of gerontology including intergenerational relationships, caregiving, elder abuse, dementia, and palliative care. What unites these various papers is an overarching focus on spiritual and general well-being that is important to a satisfactory quality of life among older adults.

The first article by Nelson-Becker, is concerned with using informal assessment to obtain religious and spiritual information about participants. This paper focuses on how older adults manage adversity and maintain self-efficacy using narrative therapy using a sample of 79 independent older adults in an urban community. Interviews examined how these individuals manage life challenges, finding that religious and spiritual themes, or lack thereof, can help professionals to reinforce coping strategies. Four vignettes were presented, which show how individuals rely on both religion and spirituality, religion only, spirituality only, or something neither religious nor spiritual in coping with difficult life events. Based on these findings, Nelson-Becker recommends that standard assessments of older adults should address the importance of religion and spirituality in their lives.

Two of the articles in this volume address how faith-based communities can be enlisted as an important social resource in addressing the spiritual well-being and more general needs of older individuals. Podnieks and Wilson suggest that religious congregations can aid in the prevention of elder abuse. The authors explore how the utilization of pre-existing connections to religious communities might be used to uncover and address elder abuse in their midst. Religious leaders are typically trusted by their congregants and are thus in a position to be a helpful resource. The researchers approached these leaders from a variety of faith traditions in order to: assess their awareness of elder abuse in their congregations; determine what resources are needed to address abuse; and what the barriers to the provision of such assistance are. The authors indicate that there is limited awareness of elder abuse among religious leaders. Further, religious leaders lack training in addressing elder abuse. Participants felt that resources needed to be developed through consultations with community members and that faith communities have very little involvement with elder abuse outreach at present. According to Podnieks and Wilson, older adults who suffer abuse are often reluctant to seek help, but active outreach and support on the part of religious leaders may provide an important linkage to other community resources.

The article that explores faith-based settings as a resource for dealing with the challenges of aging is a study on a caregiver readiness intervention by Myers, Roff, Parker, and colleagues. According to these authors, most religious communities do not provide parent care guidance and are not prepared to address the growing needs of older adults and their families. Their article is designed to improve caregiving readiness of families in congregational settings. Using a modified version of Rowe and Kahn's (1998) successful aging model that includes active spirituality, the authors advocate that programs promoting successful aging must be theoretically grounded and include evidence-based guidelines to support the content. Next, they describe the application of a specific parent care intervention program–*The Parent Care Readiness Intervention Program and Planning Process*. This intervention, designed originally for military families, was extended to religious congregations in Alabama and Texas. The intervention breaks down and prioritizes common tasks faced by caregivers of older adults into related domains such as medical care, legal issues, financial and insurance concerns, family and social relationships, and spiritual and emotional well-being so as to minimize the overwhelming nature and concomitant burdens of caregiving. The authors stress the importance of incorporating religious leaders in preparations for providing care to older parents.

Eggers and Hensley also address the theme of the interdependence of younger and older generations. However, their intervention to support intergenerational connections were between preschool children and nonrelated older adults with a goal to promote spiritual and psychological well-being through the development of meaningful relationships using a variety of activities. Thus, the intervention addressed two major components of spiritual well-being: purpose and meaning in life and connectedness with others. Interviews conducted as part of the intervention evaluated the effectiveness of the program at meeting its goals. Several themes emerged from the interviews: joyfulness and fun in being together, faith that the future is secure in the next generation, a sense of purpose in helping the younger generation, feeling wanted and needed, and connecting with others. Thus, the spiritual well-being of both older and younger participants in this intervention was addressed by bolstering their sense of connectedness to others and imbuing these social interactions with a sense of purpose and meaning. The authors indicate that the older adults achieved generative love, which increases spiritual growth by creating immortality through connectedness and hope for the future.

As indicated previously, attitudes toward spiritual assessments in applied settings are changing. For example, spirituality is being addressed by nursing and medicine settings (Patton, 2001), and spiritual assessment is becoming a requirement for hospitals, long-term care facilities, and home care providers (JCAHO, 2004). The final two articles in this volume shift our focus from spiritual interventions in the community to programs designed for older adults in institutional settings. Vance compares spiritual activities with other activity paradigms for older adults with dementia. The spiritual intervention described by Vance does not impose beliefs, values, or practices on participants, but it allows for cultural and individual diversity in the expression of spirituality. The author provides examples of spiritual activities for persons of various religious backgrounds, such as Islamic, Hindu, Buddhist, Jewish, and Christian faith traditions. To better accommodate the cognitive limitations of older adults with dementia, Vance suggests that activities requiring explicit memory skills, attention, and concentration should be avoided. However, repetitive activities that rely on intact motor movements and that are simple and engaging are recommended. He also discusses limitations and problems in the application of this approach. For example, exposing nonreligious older adults to religious activities may be upsetting. In addition, problems may arise from an enthusiastic response to the activity for some individuals who struggle with emotional regulation. Finally, religious activities cannot be easily made available to every older adult with dementia. They depend upon the specifics and severity of their condition.

The final empirical article in this volume focuses on spiritual well-being at the end of life for persons receiving institutional palliative care. Heiser, Brennan, and Redic present a pilot intervention study involving three residents receiving palliative care services in a skilled nursing facility. This intervention consists of using a portable cabinet containing materials to foster spiritual well-ness and social interactions. The three case studies reported in this article describe how this intervention addressed the spiritual needs of dying patients. Materials in the cabinet, such as snacks and meal vouchers, encouraged family members and volunteers to visit the resident regularly, mitigating social isolation and strengthening connections with others. Residents and their families were able to pursue spiritual activities they found beneficial, such as reading spiritual materials or listening to music that connected them to earlier stages of life. The intervention also served as a basis for initiating conversations about spirituality between the resident and the pastoral care provider. This approach towards self-directed spiritual enrichment is congruent with the concern that spiritual interventions should not impose values, beliefs, or practices on another in order to respect divergent religious and spiritual beliefs. According to these authors, older adults receiving palliative care can benefit greatly from interventions that address spiritual well-being at the end of life.

The final article in this volume is a commentary on future directions in spiritual assessment and intervention. DePalo and Brennan offer recommendations and suggestions based on the papers presented in this volume. They suggest that spirituality and spiritual interventions are relevant for both clinical practice and scientific investigation. The authors recommend that spiritual self-assessments and needs assessments be provided to clients in order to develop a treatment care plan to benefit the client, family, and significant others. They further discuss engendering a sense of hope for older adults and their families to meet the often-challenging circumstances of later life. DePalo and Brennan recommend that future research focus on the relevance of spirituality with regard to gender, cultural, and socioeconomic factors.

CONCLUSION AND NEXT STEPS

In this introduction, we have tried to give the reader the "lay of the land" in current efforts around spiritual assessment and intervention. The application of scientifically designed and systematically evaluated interventions addressing religious and spiritual needs or utilizing spiritual resources to address other issues is truly in its infancy relative to the body of intervention research in gerontology. Because of the historic distrust between the disciplines of religion and science, it is imperative that as this work moves forward, we are careful that spiritual assessment and intervention be firmly grounded both conceptually and empirically and that high standards of scientific rigor are maintained. Without such attention to detail, both basic and applied research in spirituality and religiousness may lack the credibility to make a strong case for meeting the needs of older adults through spiritual assessment and intervention. At the same time, the scientific community needs to become more aware and respectful of the basic human need for spiritual fulfillment. Such a "meeting of minds" can only help those older adults whom we are trying to serve.

REFERENCES

Ai, A. L., & Bolling, S. F. (2002). The use of complimentary and alternative therapies among middle-aged and older cardiac patients. *American Journal of Medical Quality, 17* (1), 21-27.

Allport, G. W., & Ross, M. J. (1967). Personal religious orientation and prejudice. *Journal of Personality and Social Psychology, 5,* 432-443.

Anandarajah, G., & Hight, E. (2001). Spirituality and medical practice: Using the HOPE questionnaire as a practical tool for spiritual assessment. *American Family Physician, 63* (1), 81-89.

Arnold, R., Avants, S. K., Margolin, A., & Marcotte, D. (2002). Patient attitudes concerning the inclusion of spirituality into addiction treatment. *Journal of Substance Abuse Treatment, 23* (4) 319-326.

Binstock, R. H. (2002). Some thoughts on a faith-based initiative in long-term care. *Public Policy and Aging Report, 12* (4), 20-22.

Brady, M. J., Peterman, A. H., Fitchett, G., Mo, M., & Cella, D. (1999). A case for including spirituality in quality of life measurement in oncology. *Psychooncology, 8* (5), 417-428.

Brennan, M. (2002). Spirituality and psychosocial development in middle-age and older adults with vision loss. *Journal of Adult Development, 9* (1), 31-46.

Brennan, M. (2004). Spirituality and religiousness predict adaptation to vision loss in middle age and older adults. *International Journal for the Psychology of Religion,* 14(3), 193-214.

Brizer, D. A. (1993). Religiosity and drug abuse among psychiatric inpatients. *American Journal of Drug & Alcohol Abuse, 19,* 337-344.

Brooks, R. G., & Koenig, H. G. (2002). Having faith in an aging health system: Policy perspectives. *Public Policy and Aging Report, 12* (4), 23-26.

Chan, C., Ho, P. S., & Chow, E. (2001). A body-mind-spirit model in health: An Eastern approach. *Social Work in Health Care, 34* (3/4), 261-282.

Chandler, C. K., Holden, J. M., & Kolander, C. A. (1992). Counseling for spiritual wellness: Theory and practice. *Journal of Counseling & Development, 71,* 168-174.

Chatters, L. M., & Taylor, R. G. (1998). Religious involvement among African Americans. *African American Research Perspective, 4* (1), 83-93.

Crowther, M. R., Parker, M. W., Achenbaum, W. A., Larimore, W. L., & Koenig, H. G. (2002). Rowe and Kahn's model of successful aging revisited: Positive spirituality-the forgotten factor. *The Gerontologist, 42* (5), 613-620.

Daaleman, T. P., Subashan, P., & Studenski, S. (2004). Religion, spirituality, and health status in geriatric outpatients. *Annals of Family Medicine, 2* (1), 49-53.

Dunn, K. S., & Horgas, A. L. (2000). The prevalence of prayer as a spiritual self-care modality in elders. *Journal of Holistic Nursing, 18* (4), 337-351.

Ellison, C. G. (1998). Religion, health and well-being among African Americans. *African American Research Perspective, 4* (1), 94-103.

Faull, K. Hills, M. D., Cochrane, G., Gray, J., Hunt, M., McKenzie, C., & Winter, L. (2004). Investigation of health perspectives of those with physical disabilities: The role of spirituality as a determinant of health. *Disability and Rehabilitation, 26* (3), 129-144.

Fry, P. S. (2000). Religious involvement, spirituality and personal meaning for life: Existential predictors of psychological well being in community-residing and institutional care elders. *Aging and Mental Health, 4* (4), 375-387.

Fry, P. S. (2001). The unique contribution of key existential factors to the prediction of psychological well-being of older adults following spousal loss. *The Gerontologist, 41*(1), 69-81.

Gerard, S., Smith, B. H., & Simpson, J. A. (2003). A randomized controlled trial of spiritual healing in restricted neck movement. *Journal of Alternative and Complementary Medicine, 9* (4), 451-453.

Hawks, S. (1994). Spiritual health: Definition and theory. *Wellness Perspectives, 10,* 3-11.

Hill, P. C., & Pargament, K. I. (2003). Advances in the conceptualization and measurement of religion and spirituality. *American Psychologist, 58* (1), 64-74.

Hill, P. C., Pargament, K. I., Hood, R. W., McCullogh, J., Swyers, J. B., Larson, D. B., & Zinnbauer, B. J. (2000). Conceptualizing religion and spirituality: Points of commonality, points of departure. *Journal for the Theory of Social Behavior, 30* (1), 51-77.

Hodge, D. R. (2001). Spiritual assessment: A review of major qualitative methods and a new framework for assessing spirituality. *Social Work, 46* (3), 203-214.

Hover, M. (2004). The role of spiritual assessment and intervention in critical care medicine. Retrieved from the World Wide Web March 2, 2004, http://www.maacc.org/_aab/038.pdf.

Howden, J. (1992). *Development and psychometric characteristics of the Spirituality Assessment Scale.* Unpublished doctoral dissertation. Texas Women's University.

Joint Commission on Accreditation of Healthcare Organizations (JCAHO). (2004). Spiritual Assessment. Retrieved from the World Wide Web, March 2, 2004. *http://www.jcaho.org/accredited+organizations/behavioral+health+care/standards/faqs/provision+of+care/assessment/spiritual+assessment+.htm*

Kennedy, J. E., Abbott, R. A., & Rosenberg, B. S. (2002). Changes in spirituality and well-being in a retreat program for cardiac patients. *Alternative Therapies in Health and Medicine, 8* (4), 64-73.

King, D. E., Blue, A., Mallin, R., & Thiedke, C. (2004). Implementation and assessment of a spiritual history taking curriculum in the first year of medical school. *Teaching and Learning in Medicine, 16* (1), 64-68.

Kub, J. E., Nolan, M. T., Hughes, M. T., Terry, P. B., Sulmasy, D. P., Astrow, A., & Forman, J. H. (2003). Religious importance and practices of patients with a life-threatening illness: Implications for screening protocols. *Applied Nursing Research, 16* (3), 196-200.

LaPierre, L. (2002, October 22). Spirituality assessment in healthcare. (Maine in Focus). *Healthcare Review.* Retrieved March 3, 2004, from: http://www.findarticles.com/ cf_dls/m0HSV/9_15/93657661/print.jhtml

Leder, D. (1999-2000). Aging into the Spirit: From traditional wisdom to innovative programs and communities. *Generations, 23* (4), 36-41.

LeFavi, R. G., & Wessels, M. H. (2003). Life review in pastoral counseling: Background and efficacy for use with the terminally ill. *Journal of Pastoral Care and Counseling, 57* (3), 281-292.

Lindgren, K. N., & Coursey, R. D. (1995). Spirituality and serious mental illness: A two-part study. *Psychosocial Rehabilitation Journal, 18,* 93-107.

Marcus, J., Elkins, G., & Mott, F. (2003). A model of hypnotic intervention for palliative care. *Advances in Mind-Body Medicine, 19* (2), 24-27.

McClain, C. S., Rosenfeld, B., & Breitbart, W. (2003). Effects of spiritual well-being on end-of-life despair in terminally ill cancer patients. *The Lancet, 361,* 1603-1607.

McCullough, M. E., Hoyt, W. T., Larson, D. B., Koenig, H. G., & Thoresen, C. (2000). Religious involvement and mortality: A meta-analytic review. *Health Psychology, 19* (3), 211-222.

McDonald, D. A. (2000). Spirituality: Description, measurement, and relation to the five factor model of personality. *Journal of Personality, 68* (1), 153-197.

McFadden, S. H., Brennan, M., & Patrick, J. H. (2003a). Charting a course for 21st Century studies of late life religiousness and spirituality. In S. H. McFadden, M. Brennan, & J. H. Patrick (Eds.), *New directions in the study of late life religiousness and spirituality* (pp. 1-10). Binghamton, NY: The Haworth Press, Inc.

McFadden, S. H., Brennan, M., & Patrick, J. H. (2003b). Afterword: A "conversation" about theories, definitions, and applications. In S. H. McFadden, M. Brennan, & J. H. Patrick (Eds.), *New directions in the study of late life religiousness and spirituality* (pp. 225-232). Binghamton, NY: The Haworth Pastoral Press.

Miller, W. R., & Thoresen, C. E. (2003). Spirituality, religion, and health. *American Psychologist, 58,* 24-35.

Moberg, D. O. (1967). Science and the spiritual nature of man. *Journal of the American Scientific Affiliation, 19,* 12-17.

Moberg, D. O. (2002). Assessing and measuring spirituality: Confronting the dilemmas of universal and particular evaluative criteria. *Journal of Adult Development, 9* (1), 47-60.

Mokuau, N., Hishinuma, E., & Nishimura, S. (2001). Validating a measure of religiousness/spirituality for Native Hawaiians. *Pacific Health Dialogues, 8* (2), 407-416.

Moncher, F. J., & Josephson, A. M. (2004). Religious and spiritual aspects of family assessment. *Child and Adolescent Psychiatric Clinics of North America, 13* (1), 49-70.

Nealon-Woods, M. A., Ferrari, J. R., & Jason, L. A. (1995). Twelve-step program use among Oxford House residents: Spirituality or social support in sobriety? *Journal of Substance Abuse, 7* (3), 311-318.

Nelson, C. J., Rosenfeld, B., Breitbart, W., & Galietta, M. (2002). Spirituality, religion, and depression in the terminally ill. *Psychosomatics, 43* (3), 213-220.

Nosek, M. A., & Hughes, R. B. (2001). Psychospiritual aspects of sense of self in women with physical disabilities. *Journal of Rehabilitation, 67* (1), 20-25.

Pargament, K. I. (1997). *The psychology of religion and coping.* New York: Guilford Press.

Pargament, K. I., Ishler, K., Dubow, E. F., Stanik, P., Rouiller, R., Crowe, P., Cullman, E. P., Albert, M., & Royster, B. (1994). Methods of religious coping with the Gulf War: Cross-sectional and longitudinal analyses. *Journal for the Scientific Study of Religion, 33,* 347-367.

Patton, G. (2001). Spirituality assessment in health care. Health Progress, September-October. Catholic Health Association of the United States, 2001.

Picot, S. J., Debanne, S. M., Namazi, K. H., & Wykle, M. L. (1997). Religiosity and perceived rewards of Black and White caregivers. *The Gerontologist, 37,* 89-101.

Piedmont, R. L. (2001). Spiritual transcendence and the scientific study of spirituality. *Journal of Rehabilitation, 67* (1), 1-22.

Powell, L. H., Shahabi, L., & Thoresen, C. E. (2003). Religion and spirituality: Linkages to physical health. *American Psychologist, 58,* 36-52.

Ross, C. (1990). Religion and psychological distress. *Journal for the Scientific Study of Religion, 29,* 236-246.

Rowe, J. W., & Kahn, R. L. (1998). *Successful aging.* New York: Pantheon/Random House.

Saunders, C. (1988). Spiritual pain. *Journal of Palliative Care, 4,* 29-32.

Seeman, T. E., Fagan Dublin, L., & Seeman, M. (2003). Religiosity/spirituality and health: A critical review of the evidence for biological pathways. *American Psychologist, 58,* 53-63.

Seeward, B. (1992). A spiritual well-being program at the United States Postal Service headquarters. *Wellness Perspectives, 8,* 16-28.

Sloan, R. P., Bagiella, E., & Powell, T. (1999). Religion, spirituality, and medicine. *The Lancet, 353,* 664-667.

Wesley, C., Tunney, K., & Duncan, E. (2004). Educational needs of hospice social workers: Spiritual assessment and interventions with diverse populations. *American Journal of Hospice and Palliative Care, 21* (1), 40-46.

Westlake, C., & Dracup, K. (2001). Role of spirituality in adjustment of patients with advanced heart failure. *Progress in Cardiovascular Nursing, 16* (3), 119-125.

World Health Organization (WHO). (1948). WHO definition of health. Preamble to the Constitution of the World Health Organization as adopted by the International Health Conference, New York, 19-22 June, 1946; signed on 22 July 1946 by the representatives of 61 States (Official Records of the World Health Organization, no. 2, p. 100) and entered into force on 7 April, 1948.

Yanek, L. R., Becker, D. M., Moy, T. F., Gittelsohn, J., & Koffman, D. M. (2001). Project Joy: Faith-based cardiovascular health promotion for African American women. *Public Health Reports, 116* (Supplement 1), 68-81.

Spiritual, Religious, Nonspiritual, and Nonreligious Narratives in Marginalized Older Adults: A Typology of Coping Styles

Holly B. Nelson-Becker, PhD

SUMMARY. Narrative therapy is an important tool in the pheno-menological framing of life events with older clients. Seventy-nine older adults who lived independently in four subsidized high-rise housing facilities in Chicago were interviewed in a research project about managing life challenges. Cases represent four types in a spiritual-religious typology: religious and spiritual, religious only, spiritual only, and neither religious nor spiritual (Zinnbauer, 1997). This article explores how older adults managed adversity and maintained a sense of self-efficacy. Findings indicate that older adults use many references to religion and spirituality in their narratives, either embracing these domains or defining themselves in contrast to them. Narrative therapy suggests that the implications of religious and spiritual re-

Holly B. Nelson-Becker is affiliated with The School of Social Welfare, University of Kansas, 1545 Lilac Lane, Lawrence, KS 66044 (E-mail: hnelson@ku.edu).

The author acknowledges the cooperation of the Council for Jewish Elderly, Chicago, IL, who provided access to two of the research sites and the Hartford Foundation who has provided extensive professional development and mentoring opportunities. The study reported here was based on a doctoral dissertation.

[Haworth co-indexing entry note]: "Spiritual, Religious, Nonspiritual, and Nonreligious Narratives in Marginalized Older Adults: A Typology of Coping Styles." Nelson-Becker, Holly B. Co-published simultaneously in *Journal of Religion, Spirituality & Aging* (The Haworth Pastoral Press, an imprint of The Haworth Press, Inc.) Vol. 17, No. 1/2, 2004, pp. 21-38; and: *Spiritual Assessment and Intervention with Older Adults: Current Directions and Applications* (ed: Mark Brennan, and Deborah Heiser) The Haworth Pastoral Press, an imprint of The Haworth Press, Inc., 2004, pp. 21-38. Single or multiple copies of this article are available for a fee from The Haworth Document Delivery Service [1-800-HAWORTH, 9:00 a.m. - 5:00 p.m. (EST). E-mail address: docdelivery@haworthpress.com].

Digital Object Identifier: 10.1300/J496v17n01_02

sources addressed in client stories may reinforce coping capacity and promote aging well. *[Article copies available for a fee from The Haworth Document Delivery Service: 1-800-HAWORTH. E-mail address: <docdelivery@haworthpress.com> Website: <http://www.HaworthPress.com>* © 2004 by The Haworth Press, Inc. All rights reserved.]

KEYWORDS. Religion, spirituality, narrative therapy, older adults, self-efficacy, life challenge, coping.

Older adults who reside independently value their autonomy and act in ways that support their independence. They retain efficacy beliefs that they are able to manage their everyday environment and create positive daily experiences even in a larger context of increasing physical frailty and emotional loss (Zautra, Hoffman, & Reich, 1997). Religion, spirituality, social support, and personal strengths are coping resources that support maintenance of self-efficacy for many individuals, though not for all (Canda & Furman, 1999; Koenig, 1998; Levin & Tobin, 1995; McFadden, 1996).

Spirituality and religion especially play a significant role in the lives of older adults and their ability to cope with various difficulties that accompany the aging process (Ramsey & Blieszner, 1999). For example, researchers have found a salient connection between religious beliefs, attitudes, coping behaviors and decreased depression and health (Idler & Kasl, 1992; MacKinlay, 2002). In an analysis of empirical studies, Levin (1994) found a positive association between religion and health indicators. Older adults typically do value the importance of religion and spirituality in their lives, with 58% reporting that religion is very important, the highest rating on a four-point scale in a recent Gallup poll (PRCC, 2001).

To set a context for building a typology of spirituality and religion, it is constructive to make a distinction between these two conceptual domains. Spirituality has been defined as connections with a power, purpose, or idea that transcends the self (Canda, 1988; Joseph, 1988). It is the "search for significance in ways related to the sacred" (Pargament, 1997, p. 34). Caroll (1998) proposes a distinction between possible key interpretations centered in the word spirituality. It may be but one dimension among the many aspects of being (i.e., bio-psycho-social-spiritual) or it may be viewed alternately as the core or essence of the person. Spirituality is the motivational and emotional foundation of the quest for meaning. Religion involves a community's formalized, institutional pattern of beliefs, practices, and values that focus on spiritual concerns (Canda, 1997; Nelson-Becker, 1999). Religion is viewed by many as a system of belief or faith and it may include functions of social support and moral guidance (Nelson-Becker, 2003).

Zinnbauer et al. (1997) suggested one typology of four combinations related to how individuals assess religion and spirituality, with some individuals endorsing both religion and spirituality, some religion only, others spirituality only, and some endorsing neither domain. Nelson-Becker (2003) found evidence for this typology in an independent living sample of 79 African-American and European-American older adults. In this study, 73% found religion and spirituality very important, 14% endorsed religion only, 5% found spirituality only to be important, and 8% indicated neither religion nor spirituality were important. In addition, nearly half of the sample responded to an open-ended question about coping with difficult life events by describing use of religious resources.

Narratives are accounts by individuals that portray their subjective experience and detail how they construct meaning to negotiate their understood world. In this constructivist paradigm, reality is holistic and multiply constructed by the person and those with whom she interacts. Narrative therapy facilitates client storytelling and purposeful questioning by the professional helper to illuminate new ideas about life experience and discuss aspects of the client's story that might be otherwise overlooked (Robbins, Chatterjee, & Canda, 1998). Techniques that flow out of this therapeutic model may include deconstructive listening—listening for other possible meanings; deconstructive questioning to help clients discern the assumptions on which they have based their beliefs, feelings, and actions; attending to coping abilities and strengths; and finding empowering ways to reframe the client's story.

Consideration of religious and spiritual themes or lack of these themes in life stories can guide professionals to reinforce coping strategies that are congruent with the individual. Professionals can help support older adult independence by exploring how these same older adults have chosen to manage adversity in the past. This may be especially useful with populations that have been marginalized as being both impoverished (low-income) and of minority status.

This article will describe the research method used to collect narrative data on religious and spiritual problem-solving in older adults (Nelson-Becker, 1999). Four cases highlighting how individuals have relied on religion and spirituality, religion only, spirituality only, and on something they name as not connected to either spirituality or religion will be explored. While there is great diversity within each of the four types across cases, these selected case studies provide clear and compelling examples of how older adults have coped with difficult life events. Finally, suggestions for use of narrative approaches will be considered.

METHOD

Participants

A purposive sample of 79 older adults from four low-income high-rise independent living facilities in the Chicago area constituted this qualitative and quantitative study about problem solving by older adults. Participants were African American ($n = 42$) or Jewish American ($n = 37$). The mean age was 77.4 years, ranging from 58-92 with a standard deviation of 8. Sixty-six were female, and 99% of the sample earned less than $10,000 per year. Thirty percent attended church/synagogue weekly or more while 34% never attended, though in an older adult population church/synagogue attendance is confounded by physical health problems.

Measures

Study participants were asked to identify the three major life challenges they had faced and the coping resources they used to meet each challenge. This was a similar method to one used by Koenig (1995) with a sample of male veterans age 65 and older. In addition, specific questions explored personal definitions of religion and spirituality and other aspects of these domains.

The four cases detailed here are derived from responses to two open-ended questions about life challenges and responses. Each case was located on a continuum of the importance of religion and spirituality according to responses to two four-point assessment scales, "How important is religion in your life?" and "How important is spirituality in your life?" Response sets for each of the two questions were; (1) Not at all important, (2) Somewhat important, (3) Fairly important, and (4) Very important.

Procedures

Two institutional review boards approved the study: one at a university and one housed in a community social service agency. Individuals were recruited at different times of day from the lobbies of these high-rise facilities. The initial refusal rate was fairly low, about 9%. Participants were paid a token amount of $5.00 for their involvement in the research, though interestingly several declined the fee because they felt they obtained other benefits from their participation. Informed consent was obtained from all participants. Interviews ranged from one and one-half to three hours. All interviews were audio taped and transcribed.

Analysis

Transcripts were examined for content relevant to ideas about spiritual and religious coping with traumatic and everyday events. Such content analysis (Strauss & Corbin, 1990) provided specific examples that exemplified the struggles and successes adults experienced with their coping. One transcript from each of the four types was selected to showcase a variety of styles. Selection criteria included reflective thought by study participants/informants.

To address need for rigor, verification occurred in checking for distortions in the communication between researcher and participant by discussing emerging themes with the study participants. A peer reviewer also evaluated the data as a second test of the primary researcher's interpretation.

RESULTS

Exemplars of Life Challenges

One case describes a European American woman who had accessed both religious and spiritual resources. She employed a religious/spiritual paradigm that gave her life purpose as she experienced marriage to and suicide of a seriously mentally ill partner. The second case reveals an African American man who used religious but not spiritual resources. He told how the "Man Upstairs," friends, family, and his job sustained him when he faced three successive family deaths. The third case presents a woman who relied on spiritual supports. This European American immigrant female described her life perspective after living in a World War II concentration camp and the meaning spirituality renewed in her. The fourth case illustrates a wheelchair-bound African American man who used neither religion nor spirituality in his coping style. He relied on his own resources and represents a personal style of coping.

Religious and Spiritual Perspective

This first vignette describes a 75-year-old European American woman who was both religious and spiritual. She detailed the difficult nature of her marriage.

> My husband had a nervous breakdown that turned into paranoid schizophrenia, manifesting itself in certain behaviors after eight years of marriage. He heard voices. I was with him for eight more years because I had children. We had three children and it became dangerous–a dangerous situation. We moved 38 times in eight years. It was a very unstable situation. Finally I moved out after 16 years.

> So we went before a judge and he [my husband] was committed to the Veteran's hospital, fortunately. They kept him six weeks. When he came home he was like his old self, but he would not go to the outpatient facility. He would not fill his prescription. So in a very short time, the whole thing started all over again. This cycle of commitments and release repeated itself many times. When my daughter was 17 and graduating from high school, I finally left him. In April of the following year, he committed suicide. Coping for me wasn't very difficult. Really, it was difficult, but you cope because there are three other people involved that you have to take care of. It was not only a responsibility and a duty; it was what I wanted to do. For a good share of those years, I worked two jobs, a full time and a part time job. I went to church when I could. We survived. I did have counseling. The coping part of it, the hardest part of it, was not getting help at first.

She reported that friends who might have been resources withdrew because of her husband's abuse when he drank. The relocations her family made also caused her to lose touch with friends. No visitors ever came and her extended family was unable to provide any emotional support due to their own difficulties. While her grandparents were support-ive, they were too elderly to be much involved.

Then she stepped back in time to highlight an experience that offered her a profound level of support. This experience allowed her to manage the previous formidable period without losing her equilibrium. The sus-taining paradigm was formed during a health crisis at a young age that she interprets as a near-death experience.

When I had my first child, they gave me gas as opposed to ether. I don't know whether they do that now. You come up from the anes-thetic from time to time. You can't talk, but you can hear. I had a very hard labor during this procedure, but it was only like minutes. I was in very good physical shape. I heard the nurse say to the doc-tor that she couldn't find my heartbeat. I was trying to say that I was here, but nothing was coming out. The doctor was an old friend. He said, "Keep looking." Then I went under again and the same thing repeated itself. Afterwards, when I went down, I said, "Well my mom knows I'm here."–There was a big circle going around.–"My grandmother knows I'm here," and so on. There was a shriek, a sound. I shot through this place and I woke up.

I wasn't awake–I was on my feet in my hospital dress–in this beautiful meadow. It had all kinds of field flowers; that's what I thought they were. Then I thought, "Why don't I recognize any of them?" In the distance I saw this curtain that you couldn't see through–it was waving in the breeze. I made my way toward that. I reached out to touch it and pull it back and it flew away. I kept try-ing to get behind to see what it was. But I knew what it was. I knew what it was. I was so frustrated. And then a voice said, "You can't come in, you have to go back." Of course I argued, crying, because I knew that everything that I thought was right and wonderful was there. Somewhere in there He asked me the question, "What about the baby?" I said I didn't care about the baby, which of course wasn't true, but it was true for that moment. It was true for that moment. It wasn't true for here. He said, "Well your job isn't fin-ished, so you have to go back." And I was back.

I can remember that whole thing so clear. I was 20-years-old. I never forgot it. I wrote a poem about it that I never finished. It's kind of hard to finish, but it's upstairs there waiting. For me, this was my beliefs given authorization. That you know even now whose voice it was. It was very nice but very firm.

Later in the interview, she attempted to locate this experience and re-assess it, wonder at it, and distill the current meaning. The meaning this encounter held for her now was different from the meaning it formerly held and it seemed as though her interpretation of the experience had evolved through time.

> The doctor kept saying, "Harriet [name changed], what's the matter?" When I could answer, I said, "I'm just so glad the baby's OK." But that isn't what I wanted to say. "Do you know where I've been?" I never told anybody for over 20 years. Not my husband, nobody.
> Being so young, I thought I must have a fantastic purpose to fulfill. I was really going to make a contribution here. I was thinking in terms of something earthshaking. You are going to turn the whole thing around to make people see what they're doing or what they should be doing. It passed through my mind, "Why did you give me a glimpse, not even a peak[sic] really, and tell me that my job was not finished?" One of my girlfriends said, "Maybe it's simply about living a life." I could accept that, but I think it's very shortsighted. I don't see how you got there in the first place. People have asked me a question that they should. "Do you think this is a dream?" No, I don't think it was a dream. I carried it with me my whole life. I think it was a gift. I'd like to give the gift back by fulfilling the purpose. But I still don't know what the purpose was . . .

This respondent had an extraordinarily difficult life yet managed to hold her family together, an outcome she valued. One of her sons began to skip school and became involved in truant activity. Through a great struggle in which she allowed natural consequences of a juvenile detention center to prevail, she was able to reclaim him and his affection. The primary problem she identified–mental illness of a family member–had multifold consequences. Family and friends were absent from her life, but her major resource was religion and a metaphysical spirituality. About her transpersonal experience, she offered the question, "Was it a dream?" and responded that she interpreted her experience as a gift. However, she continued to grapple with the implications of the metaphor and the meaning of her life. This metaphysical dream defined and enhanced her life, serving as a strengthening resource. She invested the episode with authenticity and meaning. Religion for her was a unifying thread in her life, but this mystical spiritual experience served as her foundation.

Religious Perspective

A 66-year-old African American portrayed the value of family and church friends as he spoke about the challenges he had confronted.

> The first hard thing I had to work through–I had a son get shot and killed in March 1,1969 in a drive by shooting–maybe one of the first ones. I had a hard time accepting it; it happened so quick. I had a hard time to get myself adjusted; it took me about four or five years. To this day I don't think my wife is over it. He was 17, would have been 18 in June. He was going to graduate from City High School [name changed] in June. The first thing that helped me cope was the Man Upstairs. That was the first one. Then my friends, my family, my job. It was like this. He said, "Dad, I'll be right back." Matter of fact I was standing right with my wife and his little girl. . . . He went next door to get a bag of potato chips and when he came out they started shooting and the bullet hit him. . .
>
> Two and one-half-years later, I was talking to my mother on the phone. She told me she'd see me tomorrow and the next thing I knew she had died that night. These were two really hard things I had to cope with about two or three years at one time. Mom was 56. I was 40. [We were] very close. I can say I was a Mama's boy. The same things helped me cope with both events. Going through the first tragedy with my son and then this came along too right behind it. But the worst part of the thing about my son . . . twenty-six days later my niece got raped and killed in March. My son died March 1st. I think it was March the 27th that my niece was killed. She was 14, so the family had a lot of grief all at one time. But you got to keep on going. Truly, going to work every day was a job that I really enjoyed doing. To this day I realize that people who have jobs and don't enjoy them–it's got to be miserable to go to work every day and not enjoy your job. That kept me going. My job was like a little family. Everybody had some kind of problems, you know what I mean? Everybody just getting to help one another out through their crisis.

> You see sometimes on TV where whole families die at one time. I was blessed to have my son 17 years, my mother 55 years, my father 75 years. Other than that there were the same old everyday problems. We all got problems; we got to cope with them. You can't look back. If you've got to keep walking, you want to go for it.
>
> I'm a Baptist. I got baptized when I was 16. I watch most of my churches on television unless somebody invites me to their church. I'm always glad to go. I don't have a church of my own, but I believe in Jesus Christ. I couldn't have got this far without him.

This interviewee clearly relied on the relationship he had with a transcendent force as well as his social relationships: those with friends, family, and coworkers. He underscored the supportive nature of his relationship with God by repeating towards the conclusion of this narrative, "I couldn't have got this far without Him." Although the triple loss of three close family members within a short time span dealt a powerful blow, he asserted that he had now recovered. Recovery from his son's death was particularly difficult. He acknowledged that his adjustment process lasted over an extended time. To him, the work environment was therapeutic, as was being active in the process of living.

While he described himself as Baptist, he was not attending a particular faith community at the time of the interview. However, he did reach back to a marker event (his baptism) that held meaning for him. The social component of church attendance appeared to be an attraction for him. Though he did not attend church, he took the initiative to watch religious TV programs. Religion offered him ongoing support.

Spiritual Perspective

The third exemplar was a European American female who as a young woman spent two years in a concentration camp. This event during formative young adult years shaded the perspective she developed on religion and spirituality.

> I was in a concentration camp, Ravensbruch. I was 18-years-old and was taken from France. I was in the camp for two and one-half years. I survived barely because I was young and in good health. I had a good friend–we supported each other. At first, my camp was not an extermination camp, but the last year it was a gas chamber. I

was lucky. I still have bad dreams about it. The camp was bad. It was very bad, but the readaptation was terrible.

When you are a prisoner, you are surrounded by people continually. The only thing you think about is trying to find food to eat. If you are sick, they take care of you or kill you. When you come out of it and are a young adult, you find yourself in society again. No one understands you. My mother was killed and also my family. You are alone without a profession, not able to earn a living. You want to go back to your studies but you are too weak. I couldn't sleep. The only thing I wanted was to find bread, to be warm. Without money, without family, you miss the friends that you had–you feel alone.

The experience of living in the concentration camp was very difficult. This interviewee attributed her survival to the aid and support of a friend. Friendships were important throughout her life, but she only kept a few. She tended to be suspicious and slow to warm up to strangers. She agreed to participate in the study only because she deemed it a greater value.

The camp was a horrendous experience, but the readaptation to society after the war was far worse. She reentered society once again, but without her previous supports (i.e., her family and former friends), she felt out of sync. She was unable to be at ease with others her age. She experienced a sense of alienation and loneliness, a feeling of being abandoned by God.

The French government helped me. At first I was in Sweden. It was three months until I was strong enough to travel. They sent me to a big hotel where they took care of me–food, pocket money. The doctors were supervising.

That camp–there were so many people from all nationalities. I was in jail with 250 people who were taken to Ravensbruch. I don't know from this number how many came out. We were one of the first groups sent to Ravensbruch. I was at the wrong place at the wrong time. I was not arrested for being a Jew. Gypsies, prostitutes, the camp was full of German people. Not that I feel sorry for the Germans.

We were working for Himmler and did all kinds of work. We were making uniforms for the army. We were busy all the time. If we couldn't work, we were sent to die. I don't like to talk about the camp very much.

Her experience in the concentration camp remained a difficult topic for her to discuss even some 55 years later. Death was constantly looking over her shoulder. To manage that issue, one discounted it, ignored it, and tried to keep it at bay.

Little by little I went back to school. I was helped by the government to go back. I studied chemistry and became a chemist. What helped me cope? Going to work helped me. For many years I couldn't work because of our two children who were small. My husband didn't want me to work. My divorce ten years ago was hard, but I was free. For me, freedom was always very important. That was a consequence of the war. It is important when you are a prisoner for many years–to be able to do what you want where you want.

For her going to work was therapeutic. Religion did not answer her questions about why a just God would allow the horror of the Nazi camps. So she turned to spirituality. As she summarized, "When you really feel very sad, you want to turn to something. This is when you use spirituality." Spirituality, particularly found in communion with nature, functioned as a support she could accept and trust. Religion had failed as a source of answers to her profound life questions and as a source of social support. However, this respondent also may have been shaped by painful losses in her young adult years to turn inward for strength rather than to rely on external support. Unlike many older adults, she had cultivated a personal spirituality and understood clearly what it meant in her life.

Nonspiritual, Nonreligious Perspective

The last exemplar was a 65-year-old African American male who relied on the personal resources he developed to solve problems. He overtly rejected religion and spirituality, designating them illusions that other people, but not he, may require. He instead advocated a humanistic perspective. He had experienced tremendous physical disabilities. He had become blind but recovered his eyesight. A major problem at the time of the interview was a not yet clearly diagnosed muscular disability that caused him to use a wheelchair for mobility.

I was blind in 1984. I discovered I had glaucoma and after six op-
erations I can see again. But the period in which I was going blind
was hard. One time I was carrying a white stick and all of my
friends that were close to me began to feel very sorry for me. To
make people feel better about what was happening to me, I made
them feel better about themselves. I resorted to my sense of humor.
I made jokes about my blindness and how I was able to overcome
it that day or yesterday or something like that. I had quite an arse-
nal of jokes that I would tell.

Getting to the next problem that I need to overcome is this
wheelchair. Now I make jokes about my problems here. Friends
who have known me all my life tend to want to feel sorry for me.
And I want them *NOT* to feel sorry for me and still feel good about
our relationship. It is great to have a sense of humor.

He defined his sense of humor as a major asset in overcoming problems. While this trait may or may not directly affect his physical health,
it positively affected his relationship with friends and strangers by helping them feel at ease. Being an extroverted individual, which he articulated in an earlier interchange, his own attitude improved by engaging
in social interaction. One of his monthly pleasures was getting together
with a group of high school friends, a ritual he was instrumental in orga-
nizing.

I don't know [if the wheelchair is temporary] because the doctors
don't know what's wrong with me. I may be in here forever. They
think I've got M.S. I can't get any of the doctors to make a firm
commitment that that is what's wrong with me. They can't tell me
whether I'll ever be cured. I often joke about making appointments
with the Jesse White tumblers to show them how to jump over
three vans and a railroad car. It gives a lot of my friends the feeling
that someday I'll be out of this wheelchair and be able to run
around the block maybe. And I'm not sure that I won't.

It was clear from this interchange that the respondent maintained a
very positive attitude about his severe restriction of movement, perhaps
an unrealistic hope. But it also allowed him to function to the limit of his
current capability. One of the obstacles he faced early in his life was not
being able to obtain the type of education he desired. He identified overt
discrimination as a background feature of the environment in which he
came of age, but did not mention it as a primary problem.

Daily I become weaker. Signing my checks has become a problem. I have lessened the importance of my signature on things that
I thought were important before. I have asked one of my closest
friends to sign my name to my checks. So I might as well take it
down a couple of notches, too, on a lot of the things I used to worry
about. That is my signature and it has meaning. Yes, I feel very
very comfortable with my attitude about many things. I'd probably
be mumbling to myself if I didn't have this sense of humor. I
honed this when I was a salesman. It was a sales technique.

I accept the fact that I'm going to die. I accept the fact that I
don't know anything about it. I don't know when. I don't know
how. I remember when my mother died, I got very mad with what I
referred to as God. I was raised in the church and Sunday school
and all that. I was a believer. Force-fed. I was 18 when my mother
died. I have a hard time understanding, if my mother was a great
person, and here's a lady over here who may rob banks, use drugs
or something, it seems as though she lives forever. Here's this
great person who has their life snuffed out. I didn't understand
that. Probably don't understand it now. That makes me question
religion. And the fact that there are so many. If I were in Japan
when my mother died, would I be mad at the Buddhists?

In this last sequence of the interview, the respondent indicated that he
cognitively restructured his way of thinking about surrendering functions that he used to take for granted. He also advised he has thought
about his death; its proximity is something that he now accepted. He did
not find any personal solace in religion though he acknowledged being
raised in a religious tradition. In fact he expressed anger towards a God
he no longer believed in about the death of his mother. While he placed
himself in the role of a religious doubter in this sequence, it appeared
from later comments that he was editing his comments to appear more
socially acceptable in the context of the interview. He completely eschewed religion and considered it a deception that prevented people
from looking closely at their reality.

DISCUSSION

The four selected interviews detailed above demonstrate the great variety of ways individuals either rely or choose not to rely on spiritual
and/or religious resources. Even in the case of the last exemplar who did

not use spiritual or religious resources, asking questions about religion led to increased understanding about his worldviews. Though some individuals for whom religion and spirituality are not salient may not wish to discuss these areas, others use religion and spirituality as points of departure to help them define their own perspectives.

A basic question that should be included in standard assessments with all older adults is whether religion and or spirituality are important to any extent in their lives. If older adults respond that it is not, they still may want to address aspects of religion, or their own history with it, which may provide quite meaningful discussions particularly around end of life issues. Many individuals have had religious and/or spiritual experiences that have either been strengthening and a resource to them, or that have been a source of discouragement and disillusionment. Narrative therapy can help make this distinction. Clinicians also should elicit the terms that individuals prefer to use around these issues, particularly spirituality which may not be understood in the same manner by different generational cohorts.

The first exemplar described in this article focused on a mystical spiritual experience that was an anchor in her life, but she also alluded to the importance of church attendance, seeking it out when she could. It would be useful for a professional to explore with her in what way she found religion to be a support. This discussion could suggest ways that religion could be of value to her now in her life.

The second exemplar (man) clearly relied on his relationship with God or "the Man Upstairs" as well as support from work–friends and family. Narrative work could be done to explore the ways social supports were sought when needed and to understand the ways this older man also provided support to others. The latter could be an unrecognized value that would bolster his sense of self-efficacy and larger societal contribution even in the face of his losses. While he had a context for understanding religion, he did not recognize the language of spirituality.

The third exemplar (woman) by contrast eschewed religion and in fact felt harmed by her view of a God who failed to become involved in relieving suffering. Yet she did value spirituality found in nature. Further spiritual work could include reframing aspects of her life story if needed and recognizing how spiritual contexts fostered healing.

The fourth exemplar (man) of a nonspiritual, nonreligious perspective framed some of his life philosophy in contrast to a religious perspective. He chose to reject spiritual and religious values that formed a background to his youth, instead carving out a theme of personal choice that he exercised in a larger uncertain context. Encouraging him to discuss the autonomy he expressed through personal decision-making is a way of reinforcing his ability to continue making choices even if his health declines.

Individuals seek to make meaning out of their external and internal experiences. The stories they tell are shaped by the context of the past original and reconsidered event, the present retold narrative, the current perspective of the storyteller, and his or her perception of the story the listener may want to hear. As a result of all of these variables, narratives are shaped and changed through time and place but can provide a powerful ingredient for new meaning to evolve. Problem-saturated narratives are common in the lives of older adults and provide a rich resource for present coping strategies as therapists help transform old meanings.

The typology of coping styles discussed in this paper are useful in identifying how individuals relate to spiritual and religious domains. The basic assessment question to determine whether religion and spirituality are valued should first be presented, with the response suggesting which of the four types most clearly resonated with an individual's practical philosophy. The following three questions would then help clients expand their understanding of ways spiritual and religious coping narratives may continue to be sources of healing, growth, and well-being. The questions take a funneling approach:

- Could you tell me a story about how you have coped in the past? What role has religion or spirituality played in your ability to cope?
- What spiritually or religiously based strategies, rituals, or actions have helped you cope with times of difficulty or to experience healing or growth?
- What particular religious or spiritual strength may help your current problem or difficulty?

Future work can be done with this taxonomy to develop and refine narrative interventions with older adults in the area of religion and spirituality. Much work has been done in generating spiritual assessment protocols (Fitchett, 1993; Hodge, 2001; Sulmasy, 2002) but less development has occurred in generating intervention techniques helpful to practitioners in eliciting spiritual and religious strengths. The multidimensional character of religion and spirituality imply many opportunities for further enhancement to interventive frameworks.

This paper has suggested only a few of the ways that spiritual assessment may be useful together with narrative therapy. The stories detailed here by marginalized older adults stand as powerful witnesses to the deep calling within to find meaning and purpose in life and to find a context to understand difficult events and times. Spirituality and religion may serve as robust resources for some individuals in facing new challenges of aging well in the second half of life.

REFERENCES

Canda, E. R., & Furman, L. D. (1999). *Spiritual diversity in social work practice: The heart of helping.* New York: The Free Press.

Fitchett, G. (1993). *Assessing spiritual needs: A guide for caregivers.* Minneapolis: Augsburg Press.

Hodge, D. R. (2001). Spiritual Assessment: A review of major qualitative methods and a new framework for assessing spirituality. *Social Work, 46* (3), 203-214.

Idler, E. L., & Kasl, S. V. (1992). Religion, disability, depression, and the timing of death. *American Journal of Sociology, 97,* 1052-1079.

Koenig, H. G. (1998). *Handbook of religion and mental health.* San Diego: Academic Press.

Koenig, H. G., Cohen, H. J., Blazer, D. G., Kudler, H. S., Krishnan, K. R., & Sibert, T. E. (1995). Religious coping and cognitive symptoms of depression in elderly medical patients. *Psychosomatics, 36* (4), 369-375.

Levin, J. S. (1994). Religion and health: Is there an association, is it valid, and is it causal? *Social Science and Medicine, 38,* 1475-1482.

Levin, J. S., & Tobin, S. S. (1995). Religion and psychological well-being. In M. A. Kimble, S. H. McFadden, J. W. Ellor, and J. J. Seeber (Eds.), *Aging, spirituality, and religion: A handbook* (pp. 30-46). Minneapolis: Fortress Press.

MacKinlay, E. (2002). Health, healing and wholeness in frail elderly people. *Journal of Religious Gerontology, 13,* 25-34.

McFadden, S. (1996). Religion, spirituality, and aging. In J. E. Birren and K.W. Schaie (Eds.), *Handbook of the psychology of aging* (pp. 162-172). San Diego: Academic Press.

Nelson-Becker, H. B. (1999). Spiritual and religious problem-solving in older adults: Mechanisms for managing life challenge (Doctoral Dissertation, The University of Chicago, 1999). *Dissertation Abstracts International, 60-08,* 253.

Nelson-Becker, H. (2003). Practical philosophies: Interpretations of religion and spirituality by African American and Jewish elders. *Journal of Religious Gerontology, 14* (2/3), 85-99.

Princeton Religious Research Center (PRCC). (2001, March). Index of leading religious indicators remains at high level. *Emerging Trends, 23* (3).

Ramsey, J., & Blieszner, R. (1999). *Spiritual resiliency in older women.* Thousand Oaks, CA: Sage Publications.

Robbins, S. P., Chatterjee, P., & Canda, E. R. (1998). *Human behavior theory: A critical perspective for social work.* Boston: Allyn & Bacon.

Strauss, A., & Corbin, J. (1990). *Basics of qualitative research*. Newbury Park, CA: Sage Publications.

Sulmasy, D. P. (2002). A biopsychosocial-spiritual model of the care of patients at the end of life. *The Gerontologist, 42* (Special Issue III), 24-33.

Zautra, A. J., Hoffman, J. M., & Reich, J. W. (1997). The role of two kinds of efficacy beliefs in maintaining the well-being of chronically stressed older adults. In B. H. Gottlieb (Ed.), *Coping with chronic stress* (pp. 269-290). New York: Plenum Press.

Zinnbauer, G. J., Pargament, K. I., Cole, B., Rye, M. S., Butter, E. M., Belavich, T. G., Hip, K. M., Scott, A. B., & Kadar, J. L. (1997). Religion and spirituality: Unfuzzying the fuzzy. *Journal for the Scientific Study of Religion, 36*, 349-365.

A Feasibility Study
of a Parent Care Planning Model
with Two Faith-Based Communities

Dennis R. Myers, PhD
Lucinda L. Roff, PhD
Helen W. Harris, MSW
David L. Klemmack, PhD
Michael W. Parker, DSW

Dennis R. Myers is affiliated with the School of Social Work and Institute for Gerontological Studies, Baylor University, P.O. Box 97320, Waco, TX 76798-7320 (E-mail: Dennis_Myers@baylor.edu). Lucinda L. Roff is affiliated with the School of Social Work and Center for Mental Health and Aging, Box 870314, University of Alabama, Tuscaloosa, AL 35487-0314 (E-mail: lroff@sw.ua.edu). Helen W. Harris is affiliated with the School of Social Work and Institute for Gerontological Studies, One Bear Place, P.O. Box 97320, Baylor University, Waco, TX 76798-7320 (E-mail: Helen_Harris@baylor.edu). David L. Klemmack is affiliated with the New College Program and Center for Mental Health and Aging, The University of Alabama, 107 Carmichael Hall, Box 870229, Tuscaloosa, AL 35487-0229 (E-mail: KLEMMAC@bama.ua.edu). Michael W. Parker is affiliated with the School of Social Work, University of Alabama, Little Hall, Box 870314,Tuscaloosa, AL 35487-0314 (E-mail: mwparker@sw.ua.edu).

The authors gratefully acknowledge the assistance of the Gerontological Society of America, the John A. Hartford Foundation's Social Work Geriatric Scholars Program, and the Center for Mental Health and Aging at the University of Alabama. The views expressed in this paper reflect the exclusive opinions of its authors.

[Haworth co-indexing entry note]: "A Feasibility Study of a Parent Care Planning Model with Two Faith-Based Communities." Myers, Dennis R. et al. Co-published simultaneously in *Journal of Religion, Spirituality & Aging* (The Haworth Pastoral Press, an imprint of The Haworth Press, Inc.) Vol. 17, No. 1/2, 2004, pp. 39-53; and: *Spiritual Assessment and Intervention with Older Adults: Current Directions and Applications* (ed: Mark Brennan, and Deborah Heiser) The Haworth Pastoral Press, an imprint of The Haworth Press, Inc., 2004, pp. 39-53. Single or multiple copies of this article are available for a fee from The Haworth Document Delivery Service [1-800-HAWORTH, 9:00 a.m. - 5:00 p.m. (EST). E-mail address: docdelivery@haworthpress.com].

SUMMARY. Parent care is a normative, mid-life responsibility for most American families, but religious communities need evidence-based models to help prepare congregational members for these religiously endorsed obligations. The purposes of this article are to discuss caregiving as a developmental task deserving attention by religious leaders; to briefly describe an efficacious parent care model for use by congregations; and to review the results from a feasibility study of the model with participants from two faith-based communities. Members of Protestant congregations in Alabama and Texas attended parent care readiness workshops, where they completed a structured Parent Care Readiness Assessment. Following completion, they were given evidence-based information on how to complete salient parent care tasks through lecture/discussions provided by workshop leaders and through a parent care CD-ROM with Internet links that they could use at home. At the Texas site, adult children and aging parent participants varied in how they rated the importance of care readiness tasks. The efficacy of interventions for participants at both sites is discussed. Implications for improving the model and developing proactive, congregation-based parent care ministries that strengthen generational relations in faith-based settings are discussed. *[Article copies available for a fee from The Haworth Document Delivery Service: 1-800-HAWORTH. E-mail address: <docdelivery@haworthpress.com> Website: <http://www.HaworthPress.com> © 2004 by The Haworth Press, Inc. All rights reserved.]*

KEYWORDS. Caregiving, congregations

Parent care is a normative, mid-life responsibility for most American families. A 1997 national survey found that adults in 22 million U.S. households were caring for family members and friends over the age of 50, representing triple the number providing such care ten years previously. The same study found that 41% of caregivers face the challenge of caring for at least one parent while also parenting their own children (National Alliance for Caregiving/AARP, 1997). Over 80% of caregivers to elderly persons provide care from one to five hours daily (National Academy on an Aging Society, 2000). Trend data clearly indicate that families will provide more, not less, care to loved ones throughout the 21st century.

Caring for an older person is potentially transformational for the caregiver and the caregiver's family and work situations. Although the negative effects of elder care are widely publicized (e.g., depression, role conflict at home and work), the positive, normative effects of caring for a parent are emphasized far less frequently (Kramer, 1997). The purpose of this article is to discuss adult caregiving as a developmental task deserving attention by religious leaders, to describe an efficacious parent care preparedness model for use by congregations, and to provide preliminary results from applications of this parent care model with two faith-based communities.

Faith-based communities are uniquely positioned to help families provide loving care to aging parents. The obligation to care for older persons, particularly parents, is stressed in the orthodox teachings of the primary world religions (Parker et al., 2004). Many Americans are strong believers in God and attend religious services regularly (Brooks & Koenig, 2002; Koenig & Brooks, 2002) and are thus likely to rely on their own faith and on advice from their clergy in addressing family responsibilities. This influence is particularly true for racial and ethnic minority populations (Jackson & Reddick, 1999; Jackson & Parks, 1997). Further, parent care provides an opportunity for challenging and/or enriching personal and family faith. Garland (2002) observes, "Family life provides a crucible for individuals to learn faith, both as children and adults. Family experiences test, shape, and deepen faith" (p. 23). A predisposition toward caring may become a practice of faith (Dykstra, 1999). McLeod (1999) asserts, "Our urge to care has become devotional practice, not out of duty, but from great joy" (p. 214). Parent care is as much a developmental phase of family life as childcare. When social workers, counselors, mental health professionals, and religious leaders embrace the normalization of parent care in ministry planning and delivery, parental caregivers can leave the margins of congregational life and step into its mainstream (Myers, 2004).

Some congregations are responding to the challenges associated with the frailty of their older members and the challenges of elder care with visitation, respite and day care, home care, and other forms of assistance. Although these signs of progress by communities of faith are encouraging, most religious organizations do not provide evidence-based guidance to adult children and their parents (Parker et al., 2004). As the "boomer generation" ages, congregations will increasingly experience a demand for parent care ministry. These factors are compounded when adult children live long distances from their parents (Parker et al., 2002). This paper describes interventions with congregations in Alabama and Texas that addressed parent care issues with interested lay audiences.

THE PARENT CARE READINESS PROGRAM

The interventions employed in this project were based on the Parent Care Readiness Program, initially developed for use in military settings (Parker, Roff, Toseland, & Klemmack, 2003). The program is intended to help families respond to growing needs for parent care. The underlying assumption of the program is that proactive, intergenerational planning before needs arise can help promote successful aging, reduce worry, and ease the transition of adult children into parent care roles. The theoretical and empirical support for the Parent Care Readiness Program is discussed in Parker et al. (2004).

The first step of the program is for adult children to complete a fifty-item Parent Care Readiness Assessment (Martin & Parker, 2003) that helps them identify and prioritize tasks. The assessment consists of tasks that a family may believe it needs to complete in anticipation of the needs of an elder member. Examples of the items in the assessment include, "Determine the full extent of your parent's health/life insurance coverage as well as Medicare and Medicaid entitlement" and "Evaluate the safety of your parent's home situation (e.g., falls, isolation) and employ appropriate strategies to increase safety." In the assessment instrument, the tasks of parent care are organized into four domains or categories: medical, legal-insurance-financial, family-social, and spiritual-emotional tasks (Martin & Parker, 2003). Each domain reflects a set of real life challenges (specific parent care tasks) that potentially comprises an important aspect of a parent's care plan.

In completing the assessment instrument, adult children first rate how important it is that they complete each task. Then they note whether or not each task has been done, and (if they have completed the task) their level of satisfaction with task completion. If they have not completed the task, they indicate when they plan to complete it (if ever). The assessment process is designed to help family members to identify important tasks that they want to complete in their parent care planning process.

Parent Care Readiness Program personnel then score the instrument and present a report to the family members. The report indicates to family members what they have identified as their highest priority tasks. The next step is for program personnel to provide the family with high quality, evidence-based information to help them complete each parent care task. Tailored information to address the unique needs of families is provided by workshop leaders in seminar sessions and by giving each family a Parent Care Readiness CD-ROM. The CD-ROM contains detailed information and Internet links that families can use at home to access specific information to help them complete parent care tasks. For example if a family identifies "learn about your parent's Medicare and Medicaid entitlements" as a high priority task, they can use the CD-ROM to click to Internet sites with up-to-date information about Medicare and Medicaid. Throughout the seminars workshop leaders also encouraged family members to consult with local professionals (e.g., social workers, geriatric care managers, elder law attorneys, clergy, and geriatricians) as needed to complete their individual parent care tasks.

Although the Parent Care Readiness Program has expected outcomes (completed tasks), it is best understood as a dynamic process that involves the completion of specific tasks and a continuous reassessment and appraisal as circumstances change (Parker & Martin, 2003).

In the remainder of this article the authors discuss two studies in which they implemented the Parent Care Readiness Program through a series of seminars in two different congregational settings, one in Alabama and one in Texas. Because the congregational interventions in Alabama and Texas differed in some important ways, the two interventions and their outcomes are presented separately.

STUDY I:
ALABAMA

Background and Participants

The Alabama intervention was sponsored by the First Presbyterian Church in Tuscaloosa, Alabama, as part of its regular fall adult education program. It was described to parishioners as a "parent care readiness seminar designed for adult children anticipating the care of an older parent" and was one of several curricular offerings available to adults during five consecutive weeks of one-hour, Wednesday-night sessions.

Methods

A total of 19 persons (10 females and 9 males) participated. Their mean age was 53, and the mean age of the parent for whom they were planning to care for was 81. The mean distance participants lived from the potential care recipient was 238 miles, and 73% of participants lived more than 60 miles from the care recipient. Overall, participants reported strong relationships with the care recipient, with 37% rating the relationship as excellent, and 58% rating the relationship as good. When asked about their confidence in managing and responding to the current and future needs of the care recipient, none of the participants reported high confidence. The group was approximately evenly divided among those who had low, average and moderate confidence.

Participants completed the fifty-item Parent Care Readiness Assessment instrument at the first of the five sessions. For each task, the participants were asked to indicate its level of importance (1 = low and 5 = high), whether or not the task was completed (Yes or No), level of satisfaction with task completion if it had been completed (1 = low and 5 = high), and an estimate of the timeframe within which they planned to complete the uncompleted tasks (1-2, 3-5, 6-8, 9-11, and 12 months or never).

Results

Table 1 presents the tasks in each of the four domains that at least 33% of the Alabama participants identified as "important or very important but not completed" or "completed but not satisfied." Overall, the items that high proportions of participants rated as important were medical tasks, particularly those involving geriatric assessments and establishing regular contact with the parent's health care providers. Also important to more than half of the participants were investigating costs of long term care, learning how to determine if the parent can no longer live successfully independently, and familiarizing themselves with resources in the parent's home community.

Workshop leaders tailored the content of the four remaining parent care readiness seminars to highlight information pertinent to the parent care tasks that participants rated as most important in each of the domains (medical, legal-financial-insurance, family-social, and spiritual-emotional) devoting one full seminar session to each domain. Each of these four seminars consisted of lecture/discussion sessions. Participants were actively involved in discussions and related personal issues, concerns, and experiences to which other members of the group responded. Members of the group included professionals (nurse, accountant, lawyers) who were able to add specialized information to that presented by the facilitators. Participants were encouraged to work with the CD-ROM and Internet materials at home and to consult, as needed,

TABLE 1. Percent and number of Alabama participants rating tasks in each domain as "important or very important but not completed" or "completed but not satisfied."[a]

Task	%	n
Medical		
Understand a geriatric assessment	68	13
Complete a list of parent's health care providers and contact information	63	12
Verify that parent's doctor or pharmacist is monitoring all prescribed medications	63	12
Compile list of emergency service providers and contact information	53	10
Keep a log of information from phone conversations with medical personnel	53	10
Compile with parent a list of current medications and records	53	10
With parental permission, contact all medical specialists involved with parent	42	8
Compile information about resources available locally to promote successful aging	42	8
Review literature on specific conditions to learn about parent's intervention needs	37	7
Legal-Financial-Insurance		
Investigate costs and financing of long term care	58	11
Discuss do not resuscitate orders with parent	47	9
Understand insurance, Medicare, Medicaid coverage	42	8
Help parent identify assets, liabilities, income, and expenses	37	7
Family-Social		
Identify signs of need for care	58	11
Familiarize self with home health and social service resources in parent's community	53	10
Learn how to help parent age successfully	53	10
Together with spouse clarify values about where parent care fits with other responsibilities	47	9
Assess relationship with parent, siblings and others who could be care resources	47	9
Discuss strategies for possible crises	47	9
Discuss possibilities concerning parent's inability to drive safely	42	8
Help parent organize personal information	37	7
Discuss with siblings division of labor if parent can no longer manage	37	7
Spiritual-Emotional		
Learn about end of life services	42	8
Identify parent's funeral wishes	42	8
Secure a video or oral history from parent	37	7
Encourage parent to amend will with words for next generation	37	7

[a]Only tasks that received at least 33% endorsement are included in the table.

with trusted family advisors between sessions and after the completion of all five sessions.

Response to the Alabama Intervention

Program evaluations that participants completed, but are not reported in detail in this paper, indicated that the participants rated the quality of the intervention and the educational materials they received as pertinent and useful. Many indicated they would have benefitted from more time for discussion than was available in the one-hour sessions. At this writing, the facilitators are completing a survey gathering follow-up information to determine the extent to which participants have been successful in completing parent care tasks which they initially rated as "important, but not done." Preliminary evidence indicates that the intervention resulted in participant's completing a number of parent care tasks they had not previously completed.

STUDY 2: TEXAS

Background and Participants

The Parent Care Readiness Program model was applied in a one-day, five-hour conference on care planning offered at the First Baptist Church of Woodway in Waco, Texas. Unlike the Alabama intervention, this conference was aimed at both adult children and their aging parents and thus provided an opportunity for members of both generations to address caregiving issues in the same setting. Local academic and community specialists provided information about each of the four domains of parent care in elder law, geriatrics, and gerontological social work.

A total of 11 adult children (8 females and 3 males) and 31 aging parents (28 females and 3 males) participated in the conference. The mean age of the adult children was 49, and the mean age of the parents was 74. The mean distance that parents reported living from their adult children was 227 miles, and the mean distance adult children reported living from their parents was 65 miles.

Of the adult children, 60% reported medium confidence in their ability to meet their parent's needs, and 20% reported high confidence. When a parallel question was asked of the parental generation participants, 18% indicated high confidence in their ability to meet their own needs, and an additional 79% reported medium confidence.

Methods

At the beginning of each domain presentation (medical, legal-insurance-financial, family-social, and spiritual-emotional), the participants completed the relevant portion of the Parent Care Readiness Assessment in which they identified the importance, satisfaction level, and intent to complete care preparation tasks. The instrument administered to the parental generation had been modified to permit the older participants to rate their perceptions of their own readiness. For example, the task, "secure a video or oral history from your parent(s)" was revised for parents to read, "provide your adult children with a video or oral history," and "help parent identify assets, liabilities, income, and expenses" was revised to read, "list your assets, liabilities, income, and expenses." Also the version of the assessment instrument used in the Texas intervention was altered to include some additional items (e.g., "discuss your family's spiritual legacy") not used with the Alabama group.

Results

A comparison of the adult children and older parent's perceptions of the importance of completing parent care tasks provides a preliminary perspective on patterns of shared task saliency within the generational cohorts as well as between the generations. Table 2 presents a comparison of the tasks that parents and adult children in the Texas seminar rated as most important, regardless of whether they had completed or planned to complete the task.

The task, "Assess and list your spiritual needs. How important are spiritual issues to you?" emerged at the highest level of perceived importance for parents, and assessing the parent's spiritual needs was also important to adult children. For the older congregants, addressing spiritual needs as well as reconciliation with family were concerns that took precedence over health care and legal, financial, and insurance tasks. Adult children, however, rated most highly a task that relates to practical aspects of their role as caregivers ("locate medical paperwork including medical power of attorney, directives, etc."). This finding has implications for congregational leaders in helping adult children embrace the importance that spiritual needs have for some older parents. Likewise, older adults can be guided in their appreciation for the need that their adult children may want to discuss the more practical aspects of care such as medical and legal documents. It is noteworthy that both groups rate the importance of reconciliation within families as highly important.

Table 3 reflects the most important tasks for parents and for adult children for each of the four domains, and Table 4 presents the four

TABLE 2. Tasks rated as most important across all four domains for Texas participants.

Task	%	n
Parent (N = 33)		
Assess and list spiritual needs	91	30
Reconcile with family	88	29
Compile a list of current medications and records	85	28
Compile list of emergency service providers and contact information	85	28
Adult Children (N = 11)		
Locate medical/legal documents	91	10
Reconcile with family	91	10
Assess relationship with parent, siblings, and others who could be care resources	82	9
Assess and list spiritual needs	82	9

TABLE 3. Tasks rated as the most important in each domain by Texas participants.

Domain	Task	%	n
Parent (N = 33)			
Medical	Compile a list of current medications and records.	85	28
Legal-Financial-Insurance	Discuss advantages and disadvantages of completing a will.	73	24
Family-Social	Compile list of emergency service providers and contact information.	85	28
Spiritual	Assess and list spiritual needs.	91	30
Adult Children (N =11)			
Medical	Locate medical/legal documents.	91	10
Legal-Financial-Insurance	Compile list of family valuables (e.g., furniture) and who should inherit each.	73	8
Family-Social	Assess relationship with parent, siblings and others who could be care resources.	82	9
Spiritual	Reconcile with family.	91	10

TABLE 4. Most important tasks "not completed" by Texas participants

Task	%	n
Parents (N = 33)		
Understand a geriatric assessment	52	17
Assure home safety	52	17
Identify signs of need for care	52	17
Complete a list of health care providers and contact information	48	16
Adult Children (N = 11)		
Assess relationship with parent, siblings and others who could be care resources	64	7
Review long term care facility selection criteria	64	7
Keep a log of information from phone conversations with medical personnel	55	6
Forgive parents	55	6

most important "not completed" tasks for the two Texas groups. The most important tasks overall (see Table 2) and the most important tasks by domain (see Table 3) were also reported as having been completed by participants. Thus the "most important but not completed" tasks represent a second tier concern for the two Texas groups.

Response to the Texas Intervention

An initial challenge in providing the Texas seminar was concern among potential participants that the topic, speakers, and venue would be used to market products. Senior adults expressed initially that they "had enough insurance" and did not need to hear a pitch about insurance or wills or financial planning. Some expressed a concern that the church might be interested in influencing older adults to name the church as beneficiary in their wills. The seminar's organizers addressed these concerns by making clear that no products would be sold and speakers would not benefit financially from the seminar experience. The response of the older adults appeared to be an indicator of the extent to which open discussion of parent care was an unprecedented and perhaps even a countercultural event and process within this Texas congregation. Whereas church assistance with child parenting roles and with childcare is normative, parallel ministries with older parent care may be met with the uncertainty that surrounds most innovations. As mentioned previously, there is also a cultural perception that finances, health concerns, and legal matters are private family business. The cultural taboo is that those matters are not spoken of publicly. In the light of these sources of initial resistance to the parent care initiative, the seminar planners devoted considerable time to meeting with potential participants within established congregational venues such as Sunday school to clarify the purpose and boundaries of the seminar event. The support of the senior pastor, the senior adult minister, and senior adult lay leadership were also essential in promoting the program.

Because the model identified a range of potential tasks with the domains of care, community specialists who provided informational content in the seminars were able to use this task specificity as a platform for shaping their presentations. Also, participants understood that the information related directly to their own task completion. Thus, a strong sense of energy, investment, and connection seemed to emerge between the presenters and participants.

The seminar was sanctioned by the congregation and facilitated by the senior adult ministry. As a result, it was viewed as a part of the senior adult ministry and emphasized the ongoing availability of the congregational leadership for consultation and guidance in care planning. Participants received an individualized care plan based on their identified needs and priorities. The timeline included in the care plan provided an agreement for task accomplishment.

The one-day format on a weekend facilitated the provision of the seminar for both parents and their adult children; thereby intentionally placing the generations together for addressing care readiness. The seminar, consequently, offered opportunities for the beginning of conversation around difficult topics introduced by the presenters and activated by completion of the care readiness assessment planning.

Several suggestions for changes in the seminar were identified in a program evaluation conducted at the end of the seminar. Twenty-five percent of the participants in the Texas seminar recommended that more time be allotted to adequately complete the assessment and cover the material. Specifically, not enough time was allotted for questions and answers with the community practitioners. No time was scheduled for actual conversations between adult children and parents. This could have been a natural and beneficial part of the day together.

The evaluation indicated that some participants required significant time and assistance in completing the thorough and lengthy assessment tool. Some participants found it difficult to manage and burdensome. Multiple tasks are addressed in some assessment items, while there appeared to be overlap in others. More professional than lay language was used in some items. Some of the items presented in the older adult instrument used in the Texas intervention omitted mention of intergenerational planning. In future revisions of the assessment instrument care should be taken to maintain the focus on the adult child and parent relationship as opposed to suggesting task completion acts that do not include the adult child. As a result of the field test provided by the seminars, the researchers will make refinements in the task statements to enhance the usefulness of the Parent Care Readiness assessment instrument.

CONCLUSIONS

This paper describes an intervention model to help adult children and their parents prepare for the developmental tasks of parent care. It illustrates two ways that the Parent Care Readiness Model can be applied in congregational settings. Further, it provides information about the parent care tasks that program participants in the two congregations rated as most important. The data presented indicate that there were differences between the two congregations on parent care tasks deemed most important. Further, in the Texas congregation, there were differences between the tasks deemed important by members of the parental generation and members of the adult child generation. These findings highlight the significance of developing an educational approach to parent care that is closely tailored to the specific needs of each individual family or to each group to whom information is presented in a group setting.

The Parent Care Readiness Program model offers a comprehensive map for developing an effective ministry innovation to congregational leaders who want to strengthen the family in later life and promote care readiness. Because the approach is prescriptive and individualized, it moves caregivers as well as receivers from the contemplation of change through the complexities of care preparedness to the actual creation of viable plans. It integrates spirituality and faith practice into the calculus of the caregiving act. The congregants in these samples affirmed the importance of spirituality in the care planning process in later years. The program, as it was offered in both Alabama and Texas, provided families with a "safe" forum for addressing what is for many, an uncomfortable topic and discussion. Additionally, it legitimized the promotion of conversation and mutual planning between parents and their adult children with senior adult ministry as an enabler.

Additional empirical work is needed before the full extent of the model's efficacy is validated. As suggested earlier, refinements in the assessment instrument are needed, and adaptations to older parent congregants can extend its usefulness. Future use of a refined model with diverse congregations and participants will permit systematic understanding of care readiness patterns by gender, ethnicity, and congregational type.

Other issues to be addressed in future research include how best to promote or market use of the Parent Care Readiness Program within a wide variety of faith-based communities. As noted earlier, in some congregations educational intervention programs that deal with normal life transitions (e.g., marriage, parenting, illness, and bereavement) are well-established services offered to members. Indeed, some churches employ social workers and/or nurses who have major responsibility for implementing health and mental health-related programs (Anderson, 2004; Garland, 1995). In other settings, offering services of this type, particularly when they touch on financial issues, represents a substantial departure from current practice. Thus organizers may need to do considerable groundwork in the way of explanation and interpretation to help congregational members accept and make use of parent care planning interventions offered through their places of worship.

These two pilot efforts at employing the Parent Care Readiness Program model in faith-based settings demonstrated that congregations can be powerful venues for enabling adult children and older parents to honor one another through an intentional ministry of care preparedness. Future research efforts should build on this initial work to assess how the approach can be introduced and implemented in a wide variety of congregational settings.

REFERENCES

Anderson, C. M. (2004). The delivery of health care in faith-based organizations: Parish nurses as promoters of health. *Health Communication, 16*, 117-128.

Brooks, R. G., & Koenig, H. G. (2002). Having faith in an aging health system: Policy perspectives. *Public Policy and Aging Report, 12* (4), 23-26.

Dykstra, C. (1999). *Growing in the life of faith: Education and Christian practices.* Louisville, KY: Geneva Press.

Garland, D. (1995). Church social work. In R. L. Edwards (Ed.), *Encyclopedia of social work.* (Vol. I, pp. 475-483). Washington, DC: NASW Press.

Garland, D. (2002). Family ministry: Defining perspectives. *Family Ministry, 16* (2), 18-31.

Jackson, E. J., & Parks, C. P. (1997). Recruitment and training issues from selected lay health advisor programs among African Americans: A 20-year perspective. *Health Education & Behavior, 24* (4), 418-432.

Jackson, R. S., & Reddick, B. (1999). The African American church and university partnerships: Establishing lasting collaborations. *Health Education & Behavior, 26* (5), 663-675.

Koenig, H. G., & Brooks, R. G. (2002). Religion, health, and aging: Implications for practice and public policy. *Public Policy and Aging Report, 12* (4), 13-19.

Kramer, B. J. (1997). Gain in the caregiving experience: Where are? What next? *The Gerontologist, 37,* 218-232.

Martin, J., & Parker, M. (2003). Understanding the importance of elder care preparations in the context of 21st century military service. *Geriatric Care Management, 13* (1), 3-7.

McLeod, B. W. (1999). *Caregiving: The spiritual journey of love, loss, and renewal.* New York: John Wiley & Sons.

Myers, D. R. (2004). Transformational parent care ministry: A resource guide for congregations. *Family Ministry, 17* (4), 11-34.

National Academy on an Aging Society. (2000). Caregiving: Helping the elderly with activity limitations. In *Challenges for the 21st Century: Chronic and Disabling Conditions* (pp. 1-6.). Washington, DC: Author.

National Alliance for Caregiving and the American Association of Retired Persons. (1997). *Family Caregiving in the U.S.: Findings from a National Study.* Bethesda, MD: Author.

Parker, M., Roff, L. L., Myers, D. R., Martin, J. A., Larimore, W. L., & Klemmack, D. et al. (2004). *Parent care and religion: A faith-based intervention model for caregiving readiness of congregational members.* Family Ministry, 17 *(4), 51-69.*

Parker, M. W., Bellis, J., Harper, M., Bishop, P., Moore, C., Thompson, P., & Allman, R. A. (2002). A multidisciplinary model of health promotion incorporating spirituality into a successful aging intervention with African American and white elderly groups. *The Gerontologist, 42,* 406-415.

Parker, M. W., & Martin, J. (2003). Introduction to special edition. *Geriatric Care Management, 13* (1), 1-2.

Parker, M. W., Roff, L., Toseland, R., & Klemmack, D. (2003, March). *The Hartford military parent care project: A psychosocial educational intervention with long distance parent care providers.* Poster session presented at First National Gerontological Social Work Conference, held in conjunction with Council Social Work Education Annual Conference, Atlanta, GA.

Raising Awareness of Abuse of Older Persons: An Issue for Faith Communities?

Elizabeth Podnieks, RN, EdD
Sue Wilson, PhD

SUMMARY. Churches can play a critical role in the prevention of elder abuse and neglect by fostering heightened public awareness of elder mistreatment, as well as providing services to families and others at risk for perpetrating abuse. This paper describes a pilot government-funded project to raise awareness of elder abuse in faith communities. The project seeks to support the faith community in its efforts to prevent and address elder abuse. The objectives are based on a needs assessment of faith leaders that emerged from a study that found that two-thirds of the 49 clergy interviewed knew of or suspected elder abuse among their parishioners. To achieve the goal of supporting faith communities in the identification and prevention of elder abuse, the project will develop and disseminate information and

---

Elizabeth Podnieks is Professor of Nursing, Ryerson University, SHE 624, 350 Victoria Street, Toronto, Ontario, Canada, M5B 2K3 (E-mail: onpea.info@utoronto.ca). Sue Wilson is Professor and Associate Dean, Office of the Dean, Faculty of Community Services, Ryerson University, 350 Victoria Street, Toronto, Ontario, Canada, M3C 3Y6 (E-mail: suwilson@ryerson.ca).

[Haworth co-indexing entry note]: "Raising Awareness of Abuse of Older Persons: An Issue for Faith Communities?" Podnieks, Elizabeth, and Sue Wilson. Co-published simultaneously in *Journal of Religion, Spirituality & Aging* (The Haworth Pastoral Press, an imprint of The Haworth Press, Inc.) Vol. 17, No. 1/2, 2004, pp. 55-86; and: *Spiritual Assessment and Intervention with Older Adults: Current Directions and Applications* (eds: Mark Brennan, and Deborah Heiser) The Haworth Pastoral Press, an imprint of The Haworth Press, Inc., 2004, pp. 55-86. Single or multiple copies of this article are available for a fee from The Haworth Document Delivery Service [1-800-HAWORTH, 9:00 a.m. - 5:00 p.m. (EST). E-mail address: docdelivery@haworthpress.com].

Digital Object Identifier: 10.1300/J496v17n01_04

materials that will meet the identified needs of faith leaders, diverse faith and ethno cultural group, and congregants. Using a collaborative, community development approach, this project aims to educate and mobilize faith communities so that its members can address elder abuse in an effective partnership with existing health and social service providers. *[Article copies available for a fee from The Haworth Document Delivery Service: 1-800-HAWORTH. E-mail address: <docdelivery@ haworthpress.com> Website: <http://www.HaworthPress.com> © 2004 by The Haworth Press, Inc. All rights reserved.]*

KEYWORDS. Elder abuse, faith leaders, faith communities

Elder abuse is a crime-it is a multi-faceted social problem that must be addressed by all segments of society. According to a national prevalence study of elder abuse in Canada, an estimated four to six percent of all seniors are victims of neglect (Podnieks, Pillemer, Nicholson, Shillington, & Frizzell, 1990). Reports from the United States estimate that 1% to 6% of the older population experience abuse or neglect (Thomas, 2000).

Clergy has remained almost universally silent on the topic of elder abuse, yet clergy can no longer ignore this problem of suffering which will grow over time given the accelerating increase in the proportion of our population that is aged. Religious leaders must become sensitized and begin to lead their followers to the forgotten and invisible dependent elderly. They must use their special talents and privileges to help both the abused and their abusers (Pagelow, 1988). Family violence experts and leaders in the area of religious issues affecting seniors, such as Koenig and Weaver (1997), have been clear in their challenge to faith leaders to become more proactive regarding elder abuse. Faith leaders are in a position to identify, assess and intervene in abusive situations to a greater degree than many other formal care providers because they see older people in their own context, over time, and have ongoing access to their residences (Boyajian, 1991). This paper discusses several methodologies that have been used to determine faith communities' perceptions about elder abuse and what resources will be needed to assist clergy, congregants and others in the prevention and intervention of this social issue.

REVIEW OF THE LITERATURE ON ELDER ABUSE

What Is Elder Abuse?

The lack of precise and consistent definitions of elder abuse has generated ongoing controversy and debate (McDonald & Collins, 2000). There is general agreement on two basic categories of abuse and neglect: domestic elder abuse and institutional abuse. The major types are physical, psychological and financial abuse. Neglect is the refusal or failure to provide an older person with the necessities of life such as water, food, clothing, shelter, personal hygiene, medicine, comfort, personal essentials and other essentials (National Center on Elder Abuse [NCEA], 1998). The focus of this current project is on domestic elder abuse.

Domestic elder abuse is defined by the NCEA (1998) as maltreatment of an older person by someone who has a special relationship with the senior, such as a spouse, sibling, child, friend or caregiver in the older person's own home. It is called domestic abuse because it occurs in the community rather than in institutional settings, such as nursing homes (McDonald & Collins, 2000). Nandlal and Wood (1997) identified a key limitation of the information that is currently available, namely, that it is not grounded in older people's understanding of elder abuse. For example, researchers have often assumed that physical abuse is more severe than mental or verbal abuse. Nandlal and Wood examined responses to the question, "What does the term 'abuse' mean to you?" and found that some study participants defined 'abuse' in terms of the consequences of actions. An example of a more subtle form of abuse is the isolation of the senior by a caregiver(s) or a family member(s). The senior may be denied access to, and participation in, his or her faith community activities such as religious services, fellowship with other congregants, visitation with a trusted faith leader, etc. The senior's withdrawal from activities may not be investigated; for example, it may instead be falsely attributed to age-related changes. Thus, a cycle of social isolation is reinforced and perpetuated.

Disability Increases the Risk of Abuse. Like older persons in general, persons with disabilities as a group are at higher risk for abuse. It has been estimated that people with disabilities are four to ten times more likely to experience abuse, neglect or exploitation than other adults (Adults with Vulnerability, 1997). Specific studies have reported higher levels of sexual abuse (Sobsey & Doe, 1991), and physical assault and psychological abuse

(Roeher Institute, 1995). It has also been estimated that 75% of persons who experience abuse have at least one major mental or physical impairment, thus making this population even more vulnerable to elder mistreatment (Pringle, 1997).

Legislative and Policy Responses to Elder Abuse

Four Canadian provinces and all 50 American states have reacted to the problem of elder abuse and neglect by enacting special adult protection legislation (Robertson, 1995; Wolf, 1992). The legislative approach, heavily influenced by child welfare models, is characterized by legal powers of investigation, intervention and mandatory reporting (Robertson, 1995). A review of these programs in these two countries suggests that actual responses to such legislation vary widely by state or province. This variability appears to be related to the type of legislation enacted and the financial commitment of the various jurisdictions to community resources (Quinn & Tomita, 1986; Robertson, 1995; Wolf, 1992; Zborowsky, 1985).

Protective service programs usually combine legal, health and social services to allow for the widest array of interventions. They require consideration, coordination and interdisciplinary teamwork (McDonald & Collins, 2000). Several Canadian studies underscore some of the flaws of the adult protection legislation and its implementation. Bond, Penner, and Yellen (1995) surveyed Canadian professionals about the effectiveness of adult protection legislation. Most thought it was effective, but they also expressed a concern that there were insufficient funds to administer the program and to provide services to abused older persons.

There has always been the concern that mandatory reporting may have a negative impact, particularly on how society views elderly people, thus encouraging "ageism" in society (Faulkner, 1982; Krauskopt & Burnett, 1983; Lee, 1986). McDonald et al. (1991) indicated that "mandatory reporting is based on the premise that the victims of elder abuse are unable to seek help for themselves" (p. 47). Many critics question that premise, and emphasize that one should not assume that older people would not seek assistance if it were available. Even if victims are reluctant to report elder abuse, it does not necessarily follow that others should be required to do so (McDonald et al., 1991).

Empirical Findings on Elder Abuse

The last two decades have seen a plethora of literature on elder abuse that has focused on operationalizing and classifying different types of abuse, obtaining prevalence rates, determining risk factors, and designing appropriate responses. The literature search for resources that address faith communities and elder abuse netted few results; in fact the absence of faith leader, faith communities and religious organizations in the existing resource directories presents a glaring gap in scholarly activity.

Faith Communities in the Lives of Older People. Research has been able to document the vital role that faith institutions play in the lives of older adherents. Sheehan (1989) states that faith institutions affirm the dignity of the individual, connect the individual to the group or community, and provide direct services. In examining the relationship between the rural elderly and the Church, Rowles (1986) found that congregants had "embarrassingly high levels of faith" in their faith leader and that "the single most important and trusted institution outside of the family, in the lives of the rural elderly, is the Church." Other authors have reported that the faith leader is often the first to be called when a family is having difficulties; twice as many elderly prefer to seek assistance from their faith leader than from a government agency. Additionally, far more older people seek counseling from faith leaders than from psychologists, psychiatrists, or other professional counselors (Gulledge, 1992).

Faith Communities' Response to Abuse. At the same time, research pertaining to the relationship between faith leaders and older persons who have experienced abuse and mistreatment suggests that faith leaders may need assistance in improving their abilities to respond to elder abuse. Clergy have been found to be among those community leaders who often encounter cases of elder abuse and neglect (Crouse et al., 1981). However, a national U.S. study that compared 14 different occupational groups who work with seniors ranked clergy as among the least effective in addressing elder abuse issues (Blakely & Dolan, 1991). Furthermore, clergy were found to be among the least likely to refer abuse or neglect cases to outside agencies.

This view seems to be supported by a study of 1,000 battered wives from across the United States, one-third of whom sought help from faith leaders (Bowker, 1988). These women rated the effectiveness of the clergy as lower than most other formal supports. While Bowker's study did not specify ages, this finding may be seen as a general indicator of how effective faith leaders may be when it comes to aiding victims of abuse who choose to turn to their faith community for assistance.

Nason-Clark (1997) described empirical studies in the U.S. that have examined the involvement of clergy in the lives of abused women. She reported that between 16% and 40% of women who have been battered sought advice from clergy, and usually they were disappointed. In one study of 350 battered women, 28% sought help from local clergy. The primary responses these women reported having received from clergy were: (a) a reminder of their marital responsibilities and the advice to "forgive and forget"; (b) a suggestion that they avoid church involvement; and (c) "useless advice" based on religious doctrine rather than the women's own needs (Pagelow & Johnson, 1988). Gender is an interesting variable in this work because most parishioners are women and most faith leaders are men. The clergy may adhere to a male-oriented theology and hold certain attitudes about women's place, duty, and vows of commitment that will influence how they respond to reports of abuse (Horton & Williamson, 1996).

In a study by Nason-Clark (1997), ministers were asked to estimate the percentage of married couples, first in Canada and secondly within their own congregations, who have experienced violence as part of their relationship. Findings indicated that pastors considered more than one in four married couples in Canada to be violent (i.e., 29%), as compared to under one in five (19%) in their own congregations. In other words, they appear to underestimate violent behavior within their own pastoral charge. Further research will determine whether these figures can be related to perceptions of elder abuse.

Knowledge of Aging Issues Among Clergy. The establishment of appropriate programs and services for the abused elderly and their abusers, within a faith institution, may depend on the faith leader's knowledge of aging. Levy and West (1989) administered Palmore's *Facts on Aging* quiz to faith leaders representing five Protestant denominations, as well as to Catholic and Jewish clergy. All demonstrated a high proaging bias. However, their general knowledge level of aging was found to be no better than that of a group of undergraduate Duke University students. Based on these findings, Levy and West proposed that faith leader's image of older people was not grounded in reality, and hence, precluded the adequate assessment of needed programs for older adults.

Similarly, Gulledge (1992) used Kogan's *Attitudes Toward Aging* scale to measure the attitudes of Baptist, Methodist and Lutheran faith leaders. Again, these faith leaders were predisposed towards a general acceptance and approval of elderly people. An interesting finding to come out of this work was the significant difference in attitudes found between the denominations studied. Gulledge proposed that this difference could be attributed to the length of pastorates, which varied greatly between the denominations. Over three-fourths of the Lutherans studied had been in their office for three years or more, whereas less than one-half of the Methodists and Baptists had been in their positions for that same length of time. The quality of the Baptist and Methodist ministers' contact with older people were reportedly less meaningful and their attitudes less positive than that of the Lutherans (Gulledge, 1992). Pieper and Garrison (1992) used the *Social Facts on Aging* quiz to question 160 pastors about their knowledge of key aspects of social aging. Their results showed an average score of 55 out of 100, indicating that there are ". . . some significant gaps in the knowledge base about aging among many pastors" and that "a high priority should be placed on assisting pastors in becoming more age literate."

Ageism and Elder Abuse. While faith leaders seem to hold positive attitudes regarding aging, preconceived notions of old age might prevent them from truly seeing the realities of the lives of their older followers. For example, Shepard and Webber (1992) have noted that ageism is almost as prevalent in local church congregations as it is in the general population. Ageism has been identified as one cause of the abuse of older adults. Negative stereotypical attitudes affect how older people view themselves and can lead to their being more vulnerable to abuse. Ageism also perpetuates the creation of environments in which abuse is more acceptable. Filial morality and the cultural concept of the family may make it difficult for faith leaders to accept that older persons within their faith community are being abused. For instance Jane Boyajian (1991) stated, "In our own congregations, we expect love and charity and can believe that elder abuse may possibly happen elsewhere. So we cannot reach out to victims. Indeed, we do not even see them." Finally, with respect to community attitudes toward elder abuse and neglect, Tatara (1998) found significant differences between racial/ethnic groups in their responses to statements describing situations concerning treatment and attitudes toward older people. Her findings have implications for this project in that the development of generalized materials and strategies to address the problem of elder abuse through faith communities may not meet the needs of all groups.

GENESIS OF THE PROJECT ON FAITH COMMUNITIES AND ELDER ABUSE

Abuse and neglect of older people occurs worldwide. The increasing numbers and severity of cases that are being uncovered have particularly troubled Canadians. With the growing proportion of seniors, there is an increasing demand to address abuse and neglect of older persons in Canada and ultimately prevent it from happening. In seeking to intervene and offer assistance to older persons who are being abused or neglected, service providers dealing with abuse are increasingly turning to the faith community as a resource for meeting this problem. Faith leaders are uniquely positioned to engender the trust of their congregants and become a helpful resource.

The majority of Canadians identify with a faith tradition, even those who do not attend religious services regularly. Only 10% to 12% of Canadians report no religious group identification (Bibby, 1987). Moreover, one in every five Canadians report attending a religious service during the previous week (Bibby, 1993). This proportion increases if one considers sporadic attendance or participation in special religious celebrations, such as Christmas, Passover or Ramadan.

Preliminary Needs Assessment of Abused Older Women

In the spring of 1998 the Ontario-based Older Women's Network conducted a study of the shelter needs of older abused women. Women over the age of 65 ($N = 106$) participated in the study, and 31% were over 75 years of age. The women, who spoke 15 different languages in five communities across Ontario, were interviewed about their experience with elder abuse and asked to whom they turned for help. Faith leaders emerged as contacts for comfort, guidance and support for these women experiencing domestic abuse. It was therefore hypothesized that religious institutions and their leaders could offer enormous support to abused parishioners if clergy had the information and the skills to address the needs of this large and generally unacknowledged population of abuse victims.

Purpose and Rationale for the Current Project

On the basis of the growing recognition of faith communities as a vital and realistic intervention vector for the prevention of elder abuse, funding was obtained and the project was started in 1999. The overall goal of the study was to increase the knowledge of elder abuse among faith leaders and their congregants, as well as the public at large. Thus, education was the primary focus of the project, and the development of educational materials and resources on the topic of elder abuse is to be the outcome of this undertaking. Given the current empirical findings on the role of faith communities and elder abuse, it was deemed timely to consider the role of education in promoting a greater understanding of the linkages between elder abuse and the pastoral role of religious leaders.

FIELD-TESTING THE PILOT PROJECT

The target population for this project included the following groups: older adults and their families; ministers, rabbis, priests, nuns, religious orders, theology students; parish nurses; pastoral counselors and chaplains (i.e., in long-term care and hospitals); and members of congregations or youth and ethno-cultural groups. The first question to address was, "Do faith leaders have the necessary information and skills to fulfill their potential as crucial first contacts for elderly abused parishioners?"

To answer this question, a strong coalition was formed for the purposes of conducting the study. It became obvious that there were many people and agencies that realized the importance of a comprehensive study on this issue. Included in the partnership were the sponsoring organizations of Ryerson University Office of Research Services, the Older Women's Network, Women in Interfaith Dialogue/The League for Human Rights B'nai Brith Canada, the University of Toronto's Faculty of Social Work, and the Ontario Network for the Prevention of Elder Abuse. The project received subsequent funding from Health Canada (Ontario Region), the Ontario Trillium Foundation Project, and Justice Canada.

Initial Field-Testing

A preliminary field-test was undertaken to test one of the main research instruments for the subsequent pilot study. The sampling methodology of the field-test consisted of a web design. Members of the project's advisory board and community contacts were asked if they knew of any faith leaders who might be willing to participate in an hour-long interview on the subject of elder abuse. From a potential sample of ten faith leaders, six interviews were scheduled and four were completed within the allotted time frame for field-testing. Participants included a Polish Roman Catholic priest, a Conservative Jewish rabbi, a Presbyterian Minister, and a Muslim lay preacher. Their ages ranged from early 40s to early 60s, and their training averaged five years. The following is an overview of the barriers that exist in doing a study of this kind, as well as preliminary observations culled from the data collected.

Barriers to Research with Leaders of Faith Communities

Several possible barriers to accessing information were discussed in preparation for the field-test and subsequent full project proposal. These barriers were present in varying degrees when attempting to access information from the participants. The existence of these barriers yielded useful information that was incorporated into the main pilot study methodology.

Confidentiality Between Clergy and Congregants. The first barrier was confidentiality and this barrier was particularly apparent in the case of the Roman Catholic priest. This was the only denominational setting in which the confessional was a part of the religious life of the congregants. The majority of information on elder abuse coming to this faith leader was through the confessional, both by abusers and by victims of abuse. This information is held in the strictest confidence, which not only limits possible interventions such as alerting family or friends or advocacy work, but also limits the amount of information that this participant was free to share. In the cases of the other faith leaders, confidentiality was also very important in the sense of maintaining secure access to the data.

Barriers of confidentiality vary among the clergy, both by personal value system and by religious denomination. Wicks (1996) provided an excellent overview of the issue. In this article, Wicks observes that in North America considerable confusion exists over who actually owns and who can control the information a minister acquires and disseminates. Wicks' provocative discussion raises questions about whether or not the faith leader has any obligation to share the information s/he has acquired in the area of counseling practices and confidential communications with interested third parties. In some cases, the law and/or professional standards suggest control over the information belongs to the parishioner or client, in other cases to the faith leader, and in still others to society as a whole acting through its judiciary. Wicks postulates that the possibility of potential charges of malpractice arising from undisclosed information raises the question of ownership.

Barriers of Community Protectiveness. The concern over confidentiality relates to a second barrier, one labeled community protectiveness. Community protectiveness has two main components. The first component concerns public perception of the faith leader. Questions that were raised relating to this component included, "What if my level of awareness (i.e., elder abuse) is not sufficient and could this have repercussions?" The second component has to do with public perception of the faith community itself. Faith leaders expressed this concern by asking, "Is this information going to make my community look as if its response to this problem (i.e., abuse) is not sufficient?" It was clear that an important goal for all faith communities was both to be doing whatever they can about the social problems within their ranks, and to be perceived as taking this proactive stance by the larger community. An additional aspect of this component to the protectiveness barrier in terms of accessing information was the ethnic background of the interviewer, and this was brought to light by concerns on the part of faith leaders on the interviewer's opinion of their efforts to address abuse in their congregations.

The community protectiveness barrier should be somewhat lessened when faith leaders are talking to researchers of the same ethnic background. This is true for two reasons. One, when participants are faith leaders, they are passionate about their faith and their community. If the participants know that the interviewer is of the same background, they are going to feel more comfortable answering difficult questions about their congregations, such as those focused on abuse. In addition, it was apparent that all religious communities involved in the field-testing preferred that their responses to the problem of elder abuse be kept within the boundaries of the communities. Therefore, the perception exists that if the interviewer is of the same ethnic community, then the information will be held within it. Although the participants logically know that this is not true and that they were participating in a research study, it does seem to increase their comfort in talking about the issue. The second reason for this desire for congruence between the ethnic background of the interviewer and that of participants was related to language and knowledge of the particular community. Knowledge of the first language of the participant, and knowledge of the community, while not crucial to accessing the information, proved to be helpful. While at the same time, in several instances, a lack of knowledge of the participants' preferred language and the religion or community proved to be a barrier. There was evidence of this barrier (or lack thereof) in at least two interviews: one in which the participant was of the same ethnic background as the interviewer, and one in which this was not the case.

Barriers of Time Commitments. The last barrier that arose was a very practical one of scheduling. The nature of the faith leaders' work means that their unscheduled time is extremely limited. In one instance, an interview was set up and an unexpected death in the community meant that the funeral took precedence over the interview. The faith leaders' full schedules necessitate that interviews be arranged well ahead of time, and that there is little flexibility in going beyond the time allotted to the interview itself. This barrier has implications for the overall success of this project, since it could also interfere with clergy being able to attend educational sessions on elder abuse.

Results from the Initial Field-Test

Perceptions of Elder Abuse. An important question that the study sought to answer was, "What are the perceptions of faith leaders to elder abuse?" The answers to this question in the field-test were very comprehensive. Most participants mentioned physical, emotional, financial and verbal abuse from husbands, wives, children and caregivers both inside and outside of institutions. Forcing elderly people into nursing homes was also seen as abuse. The one form of abuse on which there was a clear consensus was in terms of neglect. Neglect was seen to be the most prevalent and malevolent form of abuse. The main forms of neglect were children neglecting their parents by not including them in their lives, and caregivers neglecting their charges by not attending to their emotional or physical needs. The strongest condemnations from faith leaders focused on neglect of older adults on the part of children, with the effects of this type of abuse perceived as contributing to mental health problems, including Alzheimer's disease and dementia, as well as heartsickness or getting "sick to death." The most comprehensive definition of elder abuse came from one faith leader who said, "Elder abuse is behavior that denigrates the dignity or infringes upon the personal liberties of the elderly."

Responses to Abuse by Faith Leaders. The second question that the field-test sought to answer was, "What are faith leaders' responses to elder abuse?" Contrary to project expectations, responses did not range over a wide variety of interventions. The faith leaders interviewed were all involved themselves in advocacy on aging issues. They talk to family members or convene staff meetings at nursing homes. Above and beyond this response, faith leaders mainly perceived themselves as referral sources. These faith leaders *do* offer spiritual counseling of a religious nature, but by and large, do not engage in counseling to those who have experienced abuse, and refer such cases to outside sources (e.g., nuns or eth-no-specific social workers). This is because faith leaders often do not have training either in general counseling or specifically with issues of abuse concerning the elderly. None of the participants had ever called the police in the case of abuse. For example, in the Muslim community there is a Social Welfare Board with social workers available who specifically take care of seniors' issues; they would always be the ones to contact an outside agency such as the police.

One faith leader responded that his credo is, "Thou shalt not kill," which means in this case, that you must examine an allegation of abuse very carefully so as not to "kill" the reputation of an alleged abuser if, in fact, he or she is innocent of wrongdoing. Only one faith leader talked about active prevention in his community as a response to elder abuse. They were building seniors' homes adjacent to religious buildings so as to cut down on seniors' isolation and therefore cut down the instances of neglect with their attendant effects.

Barriers to Receiving Help for Abuse from Faith Communities

Decreasing seniors' isolation leads us into another area of study that was to look at the faith leaders' perceptions of barriers to accessing the help that they offer. The question was asked "What is your perception of the barriers to accessing assistance from a person such as yourself, for older persons experiencing abuse?" The responses varied. One participant said that if the elderly person was practicing in his or her faith, there are no barriers; they would completely trust their religious institution. Another talked of lack of relationship with the faith leader as being a barrier. The more the elderly congregant knows the religious leader, the more likely she or he is to disclose the abuse. In addition, the effects of the abuse–isolation, dependency, and mental and physical illness– would also be barriers. The age of the victims might be a barrier in that when they were growing up, no one talked about abuse. The stigma involved and the possibility of a victim-blaming mentality were also listed as possible barriers. Finally, it was suggested that the religious bias of the faith leader might pose a barrier in that their beliefs might be that if someone is a "good Christian" or a practicing member of the religion, then they simply would not be perpetrating abuse, and therefore the victim is mistaken.

Needs Assessment of Educational Materials and Dissemination

The final phase of the study dealt with material development and dissemination. The participants were initially asked what they thought would be helpful in the way of education for themselves, their elderly congregants and their community at large on the issue of elder abuse. They listed two possibilities: the first was education for the community at large on "what is elder abuse?" and the second was education aimed at the elderly congregants on the same question. Interestingly, no one mentioned materials aimed at the religious leaders themselves.

Qualifying both possibilities for education was the importance of the materials being culturally sensitive, including being produced in the preferred language of the seniors, which would be the seniors' mother tongue. Dissemination ideas included going into homes for the aged, addressing social groups, and using newsletters. Accessing avenues that already exist as forums for social and educational purposes was strongly advised. The overall response on the materials question was rather sketchy, however, because of the strong referral role most faith leaders take in response to elder abuse. Thus, because faith leaders were not actively counseling on elder abuse, they lacked a comprehensive view on what would be the most helpful materials to fill those gaps.

Due to the small number of participants, the data collected during field-testing were not statistically testable. However, it was possible to summarize some observations that stemmed from the available information. Some of these observations came directly from participants and others come out of the researchers' content analysis of these data. All participants felt that resources must be developed in strict consultation with members of the community. It was also clear that faith communities have very little outreach to outside agencies that specialize in working with abuse or the elderly. Despite this, religious leaders are often the first contact for the elder abuse victim. As leaders, they are ultimately accountable to their community for their actions. However, they do not do the lion's share of the work with this issue. Therefore, it would be crucial for the current project to target participants who actually do the work during subsequent data collection efforts since these individuals would know what is needed overall to provide better service to this population.

The field-testing also revealed that there is limited awareness of the elder abuse issue among faith leaders. Even though they are the first resource turned to on the part of many elderly victims of abuse and their nonoffending family members, religious leaders tend to have a "not in my backyard" frame of mind on this topic. The consensus seems to be that even though religious leaders know abuse is happening, they perceive that it does not happen as much in their own communities as in others. Therefore, information about knowledge of and responses to elder abuse tended to stray onto the general, rather than specific side, and responses to questions about the specific community were rather vague. One of the most important findings to emerge was the lack of training of religious leaders on the topic of elder abuse, both at the seminary level and in subsequent theological training.

IMPLEMENTATION OF THE PILOT PROJECT

Following this field-testing, a pilot study was designed and carried out to assess faith leaders' awareness of elder abuse. The Centre for Applied Social Research (CASR), Faculty of Social Work, and University of Toronto were contracted to collect data. The information from this phase of the project would serve as the foundation for developing an inclusive and collaborative response to the problem of elder abuse as it relates to faith communities. The purpose of the survey was to: (a) examine faith/religious leaders' perceptions of elder abuse; (b) examine actions taken by faith leaders in response to suspected or disclosed situations of elder abuse; and (c) examine faith leaders' knowledge and understanding of resources/services available for elder abuse intervention. The study used a purposive sample of faith and religious leaders in Ontario. Lists of faith leaders were compiled, with the assistance of the multidisciplinary community advisory board and community contacts of faith leaders who would be willing to participate in a study on elder abuse. The study team compiled lists of faith/religious organizations from directories (i.e., *Yearbook of Religious Organizations*, community directories, and Internet searches). The CASR staff in collaboration with the principal investigators and the advisory committee developed the survey instruments. In order to have representation from diverse religious and ethno-cultural groups, the sampling plan was such that 25 face-to-face interviews were conducted in the city of Toronto, and 15 to 25 telephone interviews were conducted in the five regions of Ontario. As noted during the initial field-testing, it was a very difficult task to secure interviews with these leaders. The refusal rate was approximately 40%. Interviewers had to make approximately six to ten calls before an interview was secured. A sample of 49 was eventually obtained.

Survey Results

Awareness of Abuse in Faith Communities. Results of this survey revealed that two-thirds of faith leader participants were aware of elder abuse within their community. Some of the barriers to religious communities becoming involved in elder abuse included: lack of time; clergy may be bound by rules of confidentiality; and lack of knowledge and intervention skills. These faith leaders reported that congregants' embarrassment, pride, fear, and the perception that the situation would not change were the main reasons that prevented abuse victims from asking for help from their faith leaders.

Focus Group Follow-Up to Survey

Following the pilot study, CASR conducted focus groups with faith leaders to obtain further information. The focus group participants were from diverse faith and ethno-cultural communities, reviewed the survey findings, and discussed further resources that they felt would be helpful in dealing with issues of elder abuse. The findings described below came from several focus groups. These included a group made up of clergy from four different Christian denominations and a Conservative Jewish Rabbi, two key informant interviews with two other Christian clergy, and an interview with the former Director of Continuing Education and Development at the University of Toronto, School of Theology. These numbers are not large; however, they do give a glimpse into how clergy are thinking about the issue of elder abuse, and their response to it. This snapshot will help to form recommendations for resource development.

Focus Group Results

Aside from the information generated by the survey, the focus group identified new resource concerns. These needs were divided into three groups: what faith leaders need, what elder people who may experience abuse need, and what families and communities may need.

What Further Resources Do Faith Leaders Need? Focus group leaders identified a number of resources that would be helpful in addressing the problem of elder abuse in their congregations. These included: a support group or network for faith leaders who work with these issues; a database for resources specific and related to elder abuse; a brochure or pamphlet that is condensed and that defines elder abuse, lists resources, and offers crisis and other service phone numbers (an example of this resource material already exists for women who are victims of violence); and videotapes or brochures that illustrate intervention/counseling techniques in working with elder abuse.

What Do Elder People Who May Experience Abuse Need? These faith leaders also noted several avenues for meeting the needs of older people who may have been the victims of abuse. For example, a large education/prevention campaign could be conducted. This would include Toronto transit posters, daytime television advertisements, posters in bingo halls and community centers, as well as other places older people frequent. Faith leaders also suggested legislation similar to child protection legislation except geared for the elderly. Some localities in the United States and Canada already have such law. Another idea was to put information and crisis phone numbers on business cards, which elderly people could discretely pick up and put in their wallet or purse. Furthermore, all of these aforementioned materials must be culturally sensitive and in large print.

What Do Families and the Community Need? A number of suggestions were made regarding resources for the larger community. These included a large advertisement campaign to target two different audiences: the perpetrator–(i.e., "Is this elder abuse?"); and the victim (i.e., "Are you being abused?"). Other recommendations included educating the faith community at the place of worship during a service. This could be done after a service, or during the service in the form of a guest speaker. Faith leaders also suggested strengthening supports for the caregivers of the elderly. This issue addresses prevention in terms of support for caregivers so they don't become stressed, frustrated or reactive, and would reduce the risk of abuse.

How Can Community Services to Address Abuse Be Improved? The last area of concern explored by the focus group concerned community services. The group was asked if they had any recommendations or suggestions for services that address elder abuse. The group agreed that more services need to be made available in terms of counseling, prevention, and support. They also emphasized that updated information was often difficult to obtain and that services that may have been around last month are now gone. The need for an online database that would be regularly updated was suggested. Culturally sensitive services were emphasized as being important for many of the elderly who come from different ethno-cultural communities. The information obtained from this research proved to be vital in the preparation of written materials and resources for faith leaders and their congregations.

Focus Group Perceptions on Elder Abuse

The following represents additional data collection that was undertaken to elicit a greater understanding of faith leader perceptions. Clergy participants said that it was important for them to gauge the extent of elder abuse within their communities. They were aware that elder abuse exists, especially in immigrant communities where the elderly and caregivers are under enormous stress from isolation due to language and socioeconomic barriers. They felt that it was their obligation to follow-up and follow through when they became aware of elder abuse. However, the barrier to this response was that many clergy do not hear about abuse first hand. Most participants agreed with the statement of one priest, "I still think it's [elder abuse] hard for people to name and I think it's harder to do it in church."

Why is it harder for people to name abuse in church? One priest submitted that there is a prominent religious cultural value that "It is better to give than to receive." It is hard in this cultural milieu to name that one is not being cared for or valued. This especially holds true for women. Women also tend to blame themselves when they are the victims of abuse. Concurrently, the church places a stress on respecting the elderly. For someone to come out and say that there are people in his or her family that do not honor older adults is very difficult. In effect, it means "My child or my niece or my nephew or somebody is really violating the Torah, the Bible, or the Koran." The question becomes, how do you create a culture in a religious congregation where people can feel safe and secure to be able to say "This is my experience." In addition, how does one create a climate for clergy to feel comfortable enough to go and ask the question, "Are you being abused?"

Challenges for Faith Leaders

Clergy seem to need to define for themselves what their role is in regards to responding to, or seeking out social problems. The following are two illustrative quotes from the focus group participants:

> My bishop said to me that he believes it is a ministry of reluctance. A lot of clergy do not like ministry to the elderly whether it's in institutions or at home . . .

> Social service agencies and religious institutions are feeling overwhelmed. Religious institutions, because of our tradition to say,

"We're there to help people in need and our tremendous emphasis on love and kindness and all of that, we as clergy, feel terribly guilty when we're not able to do these things and I don't know one member of the rabbinate who is good at being able to say, 'Well, I would like to help, but'. . ."

This desire to help can be thwarted by a *perceived* desire on the part of the congregation to have a place of refuge and sanctuary in a place of worship. This perception can stop clergy from approaching people who may be in need, despite their feelings of obligation and their desire to do so. Another reality that can stop clergy from reaching out to the elderly is that many times, the clergy have no contact with the elderly churchgoer's family if the rest of the family is not coming to church. If the clergy wants to intervene with a family member, they are faced with connecting with someone whom they do not know and who does not know them. The clergy struggle in terms of pastoral care, about when it is appropriate to intervene in a context where family tends not to see the church as a "player." One clergy participant said, "I think that we've been somewhat reluctant to play an advocacy role and the parishioners seem reluctant to say, I have a relationship with a minister here that may be helpful to you in the event that I have to move or I break my hip."

The issue of privacy is another formidable barrier for clergy to overcome. This barrier can be present in the value system of either the elderly person or the caregiver, or both. One participant talked about the elders in his church being intensely private. There is an apartment building right next to his church where a lot of his older parishioners reside. All the neighbors will say, "Well, something's got to be done," and he says, "O.K. are you prepared to be involved in intervention?" The response is "No." In that case, how does one decide when it is appropriate for the church to intervene?

Another barrier to the clergy intervening is that, sometimes, both the abuser and the abused are part of the same congregation. The clergy has an obligation to both of them. One parishioner is talking about another parishioner, who may or may not be a close blood relative. Who should be believed? Encouraging family members to uncover abuse on another family member's part is also problematic because it turns family members against each other in the eyes of the church, even though abuse is involved.

Time constraints are also a barrier to clergy intervention in elder abuse. One clergy talked about how it, ". . . is a heck of a lot more important to try to figure out how we're going to address abuse in the lives of our community than put 57 hours into bazaar planning, which is the reason that people like me feel we're really overworked. It's because of the bazaar." When directly asked if clergy would be willing to go to a day-long conference and talk about some of these barriers and how to intervene in elder abuse issues, no one said "yes." One participant said, "I don't know. To go to a conference feels like you've really got to reorganize your life in a big way. However, to go to a half-day, something or other is a lot more doable. Or, clergy would come to something where it can hook into something ongoing and established, like this annual clergy appreciation day." This response speaks to not just time restraints, but how the issue of elder abuse is not an extremely high priority at this time, that is, not high enough to "reorganize your life."

NEEDED RESOURCES TO COMBAT ABUSE

As materials development was one of the major objectives at the time of the focus group, the participants were asked about what they would like to see in the way of resources developed for them. There were some resources that the clergy indicated would be helpful, when asked to think about the possibilities.

Educational Resources on What Constitutes Abuse

An understanding of elder abuse was identified as being crucial before being able to respond to it. This understanding could come in the way of definitions of elder abuse and identification of the signs of elder abuse. Pamphlets or videos were both mentioned as a way to put this information out. Another helpful resource that was recommended by participants was a best practice guideline that would be, ". . . helpful for clergy in sort of wrestling with the problems and figuring out a way to do that so you're not betraying anyone in terms of your role as this person's faith leader." A pamphlet for youth was also identified as being helpful to get the message of elder abuse out to the parents. Role-playing or some sort of theatrical presentation was also cited as being a possible resource option that has proved to be effective at raising awareness of abuse issues (e.g., St. Christopher House Players in Toronto).

Religious Resources to Address Abuse

Another identified resource was the research of religious references that could be used in discussing the issue of elder abuse. "Sermonettes" were mentioned as being a possibility, where someone does the work for the rabbi or the priest and writes something that he or she can deliver on the subject from the pulpit. Another area of research would be anecdotes that could be used in relation to elder abuse. These resources could be put together with other source material and make up a resource kit that the clergy could draw upon to raise awareness of the issue. The difference in preaching methodologies in different Christian denominations as well as Jewish and other traditions was raised as a possible barrier to the utilization of such a resource. One participant said, "I think you're probably better, instead of thinking of it as one document, thinking of it with multiple quotations or multiple documents for different faith communities."

Need for Training on Abuse Issues

Without exception, clergy admitted that training in the issue of elder abuse was extremely limited within formal seminaries, rabbinical schools and theological programs. Dr. William Lord of the University of Toronto, School of Theology (1999), said that there is a standard course in pastoral care in the theological school. One module in this course is on gerontology. Within that module, a brief mention of elder abuse does occur. He did not anticipate a change in this curriculum in the near future, as the emphasis in the school is academic in nature, focusing more on religious contexts than pastoral care. The bulk of any learning in pastoral care comes when clergy meet a problem face-to-face. However, when they do meet the problem face-to-face, how will they know what to do? Dr. Lord suggested that on-going training takes the form of being able to call and consult with an outside contact. This contact would have expertise in elder abuse and would be sympathetic to the fact that the caller is a leader in a religious community. This contact could support any written documents that the clergy had at his or her disposal. He also mentioned that it would be very easy to distribute a pamphlet about elder abuse to a graduating class or to students starting their internship.

One of the clergy in the focus group mentioned that a natural dissemination vehicle and opportunity for training may come in the form of seminars in "zones" or ministerial groups in which clergy get together to explore and educate one another. Another participant mentioned that post-seminary programs would be a more effective vehicle for training because the "theological programs feel like they're always being asked to save the world and they're just trying to make sure that they can train a few people and get them out there." The consensus amongst all of the people interviewed was that more training needed to happen, but that it would be a hard sell if clergy were not personally involved in the issue. If this is true, it explains why clergy may be somewhat hesitant to buy into an education and awareness program that would increase their exposure to the issue without increasing their training. The problem is: "What comes first, the chicken or the egg?" They cannot respond without training and they are hesitant to obtain training because of the above barriers, including lack of priority due to a lack of personal involvement in the issue.

RECOMMENDATIONS FOR NEXT STEPS WITH FAITH LEADERS

Existing groups of clergy in which education and awareness activities are taking place-such as "zone" meetings, ministerial groups, Dioceses' committee meetings, and clergy appreciation days–may be promising avenues to promote outreach and education to faith leaders around elder abuse. The purpose of such contacts would be to facilitate discussion and resolution on the following areas: the role of the clergy in responding to social concerns such as elder abuse; how to create a religious culture where people feel comfortable talking about or disclosing elder abuse; determining what would be needed to increase the priority of addressing elder abuse for individual religious congregations as well as umbrella networks such as diocesan offices. In terms of ideas regarding resources that would be helpful to clergy, these included putting out a call to clergy, parishioners, researchers and seminary students to uncover anecdotes and religious references to be used in sermonettes that can be given by clergy from the pulpit to address the topic of elder abuse. Additionally, modifying the module on gerontology in the theological seminary to make the section on elder abuse more relevant to the students (i.e., talking about the problems regarding the role of clergy in responding to the issue and/or the "chicken and the egg" scenario).

PROMOTING EDUCATION ON ELDER ABUSE

Education is one of the most significant primary prevention interventions in elder abuse (Podnieks & Baillie, 1995). It is essential that older adults have information to help understand their rights and to assist in finding help. Education empowers older parishioners of faith communities and aids them in understanding information that may be provided by their faith leader. Education also prepares faith leaders to intervene with greater understanding when congregants disclose abuse.

Self-education, participation in seminars, and the development of resources and strategies for the faith community as a whole are all ways to assist faith leaders to increase their knowledge of aging. Some training projects in the past, targeting faith leaders, have resulted in improving knowledge about a certain issue, such as caregiving to the elderly, and stimulated the development of programs aimed at helping with that issue (Sheehan, 1989). Faith leaders are extremely busy people due to their dynamic role. As a result, some educators have reported faith leaders signaling their interest in training programs by sending church-affiliated designees rather than attending themselves (Sheehan, 1989). This can make faith leaders a difficult group to target for training, particularly if the goal is to increase the faith leaders' knowledge about a particular topic, such as aging or elder abuse and neglect.

Youngman (1989) reports that significant differences have been found between clergy and lay religious leaders when it comes to increasing their knowledge about older persons within the context of a Planned Learning Experience (PLE). The PLE that Youngman examined was a one-day activity called "Workshops for Religious Leadership on Aging" and included such topics as "Becoming Aware of the Aging Process," "Realities of Aging," "Aging and the Religious Community," and "Program Building in Your Congregation." After the PLE was conducted, it was found that clergy's knowledge had increased significantly while that of the lay leaders had not. Youngman hypothesized that the difference may have been due to several factors, such as the clergy's greater motivation to learn, the greater extent of the clergy's prior formal education and the clergy's greater need to learn. On the other hand, clergy's positive and negative beliefs were not changed by the PLE, whereas lay leaders' positive beliefs rose significantly. The nature of the PLE is thought to have been responsible for this difference. For example, the information was presented to groups as opposed to single persons. Youngman points out that group listening has been found to be more effective at changing beliefs than solitary listening if the majority of the group favors the position taken by the communicator. As well, one-sided presentations have been found to be more effective at changing the beliefs of less-well-educated people, which in this case were the lay leaders (Youngman, 1989). Finally, characteristics of the presenter, such as being seen as credible and as a member of the group, were thought to play an important role in the findings.

Educational sessions such as PLEs may be more effective in changing faith leaders' knowledge and beliefs if they are sponsored by specific denominations. For the present, this supports the importance attached to the involvement and participation of faith leaders in all aspects of the study, particularly in the development of educational·resources and strategies. A second point to consider is discussed by Pieper and Garrison (1992). That is, due to realities of pastoral life, educational initiatives targeting faith institutions are perhaps better structured when there is a minimal time investment involved, and such initiatives occur as part of the regular ongoing professional activities of the faith leader.

In some incidences, written materials arriving on the doorsteps of faith leaders could prove to be a practical and cost-effective way of getting the maximum amount of information to the maximum number of faith leaders. This strategy would also eliminate the dependence on their felt sense to become more knowledgeable about elder abuse, motivating them to seek out information on their own (Pieper & Garrison, 1992). These materials could take the form of elder abuse information columns in newsletters and journals regularly delivered to faith leaders, or separate monthly newsletters devoted exclusively to the issue of elder abuse.

Nichols (1995) highlights an additional component of successfully targeting faith leaders for training–collaboration with community agencies. One of the three most important factors that leads to the development of more aging programs within a faith institution is their collaboration with community agencies (Sheehan et al., 1988). It was with this in mind that the "Churches in Rural Aging Networks: Education and Collaborative Efforts" (CRANCE) project was developed. CRANCE is a continuing education project involving West Virginia University Gerontology Center, the West Virginia Council of Churches and the West Virginia Commission on Aging. The program was created in order to respond to rural area clergy who were being faced with an increasingly larger group of older parishioners, but reported inadequate training in ministry to the elderly. Congregations with high percentages of elderly tend to be in the inner city, central city or rural areas (Nichols, 1995). The large-scale collaboration described by Nichols is perhaps beyond the scope of the Ontario project; however, the content of the workshops and educational materials merit further investigation. Workshops were held on such topics as "Social Issues of Aging," "Health/ Physical Issues of Aging," "Myths about Aging," and "Church Ministries for Older Adults." Elder abuse education could be easily integrated into all of these topics. In the end, CRANCE was successful in motivating the development of even more collaborative projects between local faith institutions and community agencies.

TAKING THE DIALOGUE FORWARD

In reviewing the literature, other areas of discussion have emerged and are worthy of examination. These include the length of time since a faith leader has graduated from seminary, and the location of the faith institution. Researchers have documented conflict within faith institutions centered on an age gap between new faith leaders and the oldest members of the congregation, who are very aware of both its history and tradition (Underwood, 1991).

One of the participants in the study identified the age of her faith leader as a barrier to the disclosure of elder abuse; he was *too* young. This conflict often arises when the faith leader joins the faith community and begins to promote new programs, encouraging change before becoming a part of the long-established system. Reasoning for the new programs may only be based on the faith leader's perceptions and not the actual needs of the older congregants in the faith community. Underwood (1991) explains that the ensuing conflict can cause positions to become rigid, and this process may reinforce stereotypes. On the one hand, the faith leader may see older members as "uncreative, self-satisfied and uninteresting as people." On the other hand, older congregants may see the young faith leader as someone who cannot be trusted, especially when it comes to disclosing information such as elder abuse.

Rural faith institutions also merit special consideration. Rural faith communities tend to comprise high percentages of older persons (Nichols, 1995). However, rural ministers are often recent seminary graduates and commonly leave the rural setting once a more urban location can be found (Rowles, 1986). As we have seen from the earlier research presented involving Baptist, Methodist, and Lutheran faith leaders, length of pastorate is thought to be related to the faith leaders' attitudes toward aging, as well as the quality of contact with older congregants (Gulledge, 1992). In other words, rural faith leaders' expectation of a short pastorate may prevent them from investing time in the development of meaningful relationships with older followers. Also, people in rural areas tend to be extremely reluctant to be identified as needing support (Rowles, 1986). This suggests that rural faith leaders may need to be even more aware of elder abuse indicators and risk factors than their urban counterparts if they are to respond effectively to the issue.

RELATIONSHIP BETWEEN DOMESTIC VIOLENCE AND ELDER ABUSE

Although we have cited the lack of current scholarships for elder abuse and faith communities, we can borrow from other fields of inquiry, most particularly family violence. Clarke (1986) offers very specific advice to pastors on the need to listen to battered women and to provide help in the form of resources and referral. She speaks of the need for shelters and support groups. Pastors are urged to exert their influence on followers by speaking about the problem of abuse, in addition to staying in contact with the battered women and to help find or maintain a connection for them somewhere in the church.

Are these initiatives being used, or advocated for, in working with abused older adults? Hendrickson (1986) argues that there must be a systematic exploration of the major issues and problems facing the elderly today and in the near future. Leaders of the faith community must be active participants in shaping national policy related to aging. Elder abuse is a health issue and should fall under health policy. Martin (1987) includes a chapter on elder abuse in which he identifies the teaching of nonviolent coping behaviors early in life as a fundamental prevention strategy. This supports the activities of this project, which seeks to include youth in elder abuse awareness through the development of nonviolent conflict-resolution alternatives.

As those of us in the field of elder abuse look to the researchers in spouse/partner abuse we find much to adapt from the work of Nason-Clark. Her book, *The Battered Wife: How Christians Confront Family Violence* (1997), invites many comparisons with elder abuse. She refers to the religious victims of abuse who have little help other than their faith perspective to make sense of the mistreatment they are enduring. This was also a finding in a study conducted by the Older Women's Network in Toronto. Sadly, the response of faith leaders to the disclosure of elder abuse has been ineffective at best. Nason-Clark discusses the need for faith leaders to be more aware of secular resources such as the police, shelters/transition houses, social services and health services. She also refers to the lack of training of religious leaders–a situation that was clearly revealed in the Older Women's Network study on elder abuse cited above.

Innovative Faith-Based Outreach

The consortium for Elder Abuse Prevention Program at the Institute on Aging (IOA) of San Francisco, a former partner and now consultant to the National Center on Elder Abuse, has just launched a national initiative to share ideas on involving and creating relationships with communities of faith. In San Francisco, faith congregations have always been part of the IOA's outreach efforts. At the beginning of 2003, however, the IOA began to target this group due to a change in California law (*AB:255*) that legally required all clergy in the state to report elder/dependant adult abuse. With funding from the National Center on Elder Abuse, the efforts in San Francisco included: partnering with the city's Inter-Faith Council to create a database of all faith congregations in the city; sending a notice of the new mandated reporting law to each of these congregations; offering a free training seminar on elder/dependent adult abuse for all clergy; working collaboratively with the Department of Public Health's violence prevention project to reach African American clergy; and providing training to individual congregations when invited. The IOA staff learned some valuable lessons, through their successes and failures, about working with the faith community (Twomey, 2004, p. 2). Among the initiatives is a curriculum to train clergy on elder abuse, which will be posted on the National Center on Elder Abuse Website and will be available for the elder abuse prevention community. IOA also hosted two national teleconferences for state and area agencies on aging and adult protective services personnel to share experiences and successful partnerships with faith communities.

Parish Nursing

This paper concludes with a brief message on the power of parish nurses to link the vision of the church as a historic facilitator of healing with modern health promotion goals (Shank, Weis, & Mathews, 1996). Parish nurses provide holistic nursing services to members of church congregations. Parish nursing is not just about putting a nurse in a church. The nurse is part of a broad concept of Health Ministry, which is about restoring the healing aspects of Christian heritage. Many of the gospel stories are about healing. Throughout the ages, Christian orders have provided sanctuaries for the sick and the poor. The concept of sha-lom wholeness, or whole health, including the help of nurses, may be a useful concept for all faith traditions. Health ministry has four main parts: the faith/health connection, the church as a healing community, the health cabinet, and the parish nurse. The nurse is an integral part of the health ministry team.

The focus of a parish nurse is to promote health and wellness in the body, mind and spirit of those they serve (Ebersole, 2000). The potential for parish nurses to work with the clergy and intervene in cases of elder abuse is enormous. They are welcomed into the homes of their clients, they are able to observe signs and symptoms of neglect, and most importantly, they are trusted by both older persons and their families. There is a growing body of literature on parish nurses which now needs to examine the role of the parish nurse in working with other members of the faith community to prevent elder abuse and neglect.

CONCLUSION

People must be able to be open about their neediness, brokenness, and failure, and in doing so, to find acceptance and reconciliation. Intercessory prayer, ritual, and laying-on-of-hands promote health and healing. Sermons, support groups, and workshops can empower people to take responsibility for their relationships and their health. The church can be an inspiration for volunteering and social action for the health of the congregation and indeed for the wider community. It can be especially helpful to seniors at a time of depleted community services. This is especially true in rural communities and in ethnic groups where cultural and language barriers affect seniors.

Older people who suffer abuse and neglect are often reluctant to seek help. However, a trusting relationship between faithful older persons and their faith leaders may make disclosure of mistreatment more bearable. As Pagelow (1988) notes, while older adults may be comfortable in dissembling to an outsider in order to protect a family member or significant other, telling a lie to a member of the clergy contradicts a lifetime of religious training and values. It is believed that faith leaders may, in fact, encounter cases of elder abuse more frequently than other service providers. Older persons are likely to share their experiences of abuse with someone they deem trustworthy and feel safe with, namely a faith leader, and rightly so. Abuse damages the body, mind, and spirit.

Perhaps more than any other single resource, faith leaders are in the special position of being able to offer spiritual and emotional help and guidance to victims. Seniors should be able to view their faith community as a safe haven and place for spiritual renewal. At no other point in time are the services of the church, temple, synagogue, or mosque potentially more valuable or restorative than when a crime has been perpetuated against an elderly person. The power of a higher spirit, the religious tradition of unconditional love and care are unique aspects of victim assistance that only the faith community can provide.

North American population demographics will result in a rapid rise in both the number of older persons who belong to a faith community and cases of elder abuse. It has been reported that faith institutions may not be prepared to meet the needs of senior congregants, particularly their oldest members who, due to advancing age, are at higher risk of being abused. Research indicates that education with appropriate materials and participation in educational sessions may help faith leaders better respond to this growing population. The most effective means of identifying and combating elder abuse may well be a thorough understanding of the actual aging process. To this end, schools of theology and/or seminaries must seriously consider incorporating gerontology courses as part of their core curriculum for future faith leaders.

Faith leaders and community agencies must partner together to ensure that spiritually sensitive social services are available to abused older adults. The study discussed in this paper is a step in that direction. The information collected and disseminated through the project will inform and enlighten faith leaders, their communities, researchers and policy makers of the role that faith institutions are taking, and should be assuming with respect to elder abuse. Most importantly, however, the valuable findings of the project will go a long way to helping older, abused churchgoers by working with faith leaders in improving and extending their abilities to respond to the abuse and neglect of older persons.

REFERENCES

Adults with Vulnerability: Addressing Abuse and Neglect. (1997). Conference Proceedings, Colony Hotel, Toronto, Ontario. Toronto, ON: Author.

Bibby, R. (1983). *Unknown Gods: The ongoing story of religion in Canada.* Toronto, ON: Stoddart.

Bibby, R. (1987). *Fragmented Gods: The poverty and potential of religion in Canada.* Toronto, ON: Irwin.

Bibby, R. (1997). The persistence of Christian religious identification in Canada. In *Canadian Social Trends* (Catalogue No. 11-008-XPE). Ottawa, ON: Statistics Canada.

Blakely, B., & Dolan, R. (1991). The relative contributions of occupation groups in the discovery and treatment of elder abuse and neglect. *Journal of Gerontological Social Work, 17* (1/2), 183-199.

Bond, J., Penner, R., & Yellen, P. (1995). Perceived effectiveness of legislation concerning abuse of the elderly: A survey of professionals in Canada and the United States. *Canadian Journal on Aging, 14* (2), 118-135.

Bowker, L. (1988). Religious victims and their religious leaders: Services delivered to one thousand battered women by the clergy. In A. L Horton & J. A. Williamson (Eds.), *Abuse and Religion: When praying isn't enough* (pp. 229-234). Lexington, MA: D. C. Health and Company.

Boyajian, J. (1991). Elder abuse. In M. D. Pellauer, B. Chester, & J. A. Boyajian (Eds.), *The view from the chancel in sexual assault and abuse: A handbook for clergy and religious professionals* (pp. 31-45). San Francisco: Harper and Row.

Clarke, R. (1986). *Pastoral care of battered women.* Philadelphia: Westminster Press.

Crouse, J., Cobb, D., Harris, B., Kopecky, F., & Poertner, J. (1981). *Abuse and neglect of the elderly in Illinois: Incidence and characteristics, legislation and policy recommendations. Executive summary.* Springfield, IL: Illinois State Department of Aging.

Faulkner, L. (1982). Mandating the reporting of suspected cases of elder abuse: An inappropriate, ineffective and ageist response to the abuse of older adults. *Family Law Quarterly, 16,* 69-91.

Gulledge, J. (1992). Influences on clergy attitudes toward aging. *Journal of Religious Gerontology, 8* (2), 63-77.

Hendrickson, M. (1986). *The role of the church in aging: Implications for policy and action.* Binghamton, NY: The Haworth Press, Inc.

Horton, A. (1988). *Abuse and religion.* Lexington, MA: D. C. Health and Company.

Koenig, H. W., & Weaver, A. (1997). *Counseling troubled older adults: A handbook for pastors and religious caregivers.* Nashville, TN: Abingdon Press.

Krauskopf, J., & Burnett, M. (1983). The elderly person: When protection becomes abuse. *Trial, 19,* 61-67.

Lee, D. (1986). Mandatory reporting of elder abuse: A cheap but ineffective solution to the problem. *Fordham Urban Law Journal, 14,* 723-771.

Levy, W., & West, H. (1989). Knowledge of aging among clergy. *Journal of Religion and Aging, 5* (3), 67-73.

Lord, W. (1999). University of Toronto, School of Theology. Personal Conversation, October 24.

Martin, G. (1987). *Counseling for family violence and abuse.* Dallas, TX: Word Publishing.

McDonald, L., & Collins, A. (2000). *Abuse and neglect of older adults: A discussion paper.* Ottawa, ON: Family Violence Prevention Unit, Health Canada.

McDonald, P., Hornick, J., Robertson, G., & Wallace, J. (1991). *Elder abuse and neglect in Canada.* Toronto: Butterworths.

Nandlal, J., & Wood, L. (1997). Older people's understandings of verbal abuse. *Journal of Elder Abuse and Neglect, 9* (1), 17-31.

Nason-Clark, N. (1997). *The battered wife: How Christians confront family violence.* Louisville, KY: Westminster John Knorr Press.

National Center on Elder Abuse. (1995). *To Reach Beyond Our Grasp: A Community Outreach Guide for Professionals in the Field of Elder Abuse Prevention.* Washington, DC: Author.

Nichols, A. (1995). Planning and implementing a statewide collaborative gerontology education program for religious professionals in rural areas. *Journal of Religious Gerontology, 9*(2), 51-67.

Older Women's Network. (1998). *Study of Shelter Needs of Abused Older Women.* Toronto, ON: Older Women's Network.

Pagelow, M. (1988b). Abuse of the Elderly in the Home. In A. L. Horton & J. A. Williamson (Eds.), *Abuse and Religion: When praying isn't enough.* Lexington, MA: D. C. Health and Company.

Pagelow, M., & Johnson, P. (1988). Abuse in the American family: The role of religion. In A. L Horton & J. A. Williamson (Eds.), *Abuse and Religion: When praying isn't enough.* Lexington, MA: D. C. Health and Company.

Pieper, H., & Garrison, T. (1992). Knowledge of social aspects of aging among pastors. *Journal of Religious Gerontology, 8*(4), 89-105.

Podnieks, E. (1999). Elder abuse is everybody's problem. *Senior Source* (Summer), 6-8.

Podnieks, E. (2001, October). *Understanding elder abuse in long-term care facilities.* Paper session presented at the Provincial Faith Interest Groups Workshop, Toronto, ON.

Podnieks, E., & Baillie, E. (1995). Education as the key to the prevention of elder abuse and neglect. In M. MacLean (Ed.), *Abuse and neglect of older Canadians: Strategies for Change* (pp. 81-93). Toronto, ON: Canadian Association on Gerontology.

Podnieks, E., Pillemer, K., Nicholson, J., Shilington, T., & Fritzell, A. (1990). *National survey on abuse of the elderly in Canada.* Toronto, ON: Ryerson Polytechnic University.

Pringle, D. (1997). Who is at risk? In *Adults with vulnerability: Addressing Abuse and Neglect* (Conference Proceedings, pp. 3-6). Toronto, ON: Adults with Vulnerability: Addressing Abuse and Neglect.

Quinn, M., & Tomita, S. (1986). *Elder abuse and neglect: Causes, diagnosis, and intervention strategies.* New York: Springer.

Robertson, G. (1995). Legal approaches to elder abuse and neglect. In M. J. MacLean (Ed.), *Abuse and Neglect of Older Canadians: Strategies for Change* (pp. 55-62). Toronto, ON: Thompson Educational Publishing, Inc.

Roeher Institute. (1995). *Harm's Way: The many faces of violence and abuse against people with disabilities in Canada.* Toronto, ON: Author, York University.

Rowles, G. (1986). The rural elderly and the church. *Journal of Religion and Aging, 2*(1/2), 79-97.

Sheehan, N. (1989). The caregiver information project: A mechanism to assist religious leaders to help family caregivers. *The Gerontologist, 29* (5), 703-709.

Shepard, G., & Webber, J. (1992). Life satisfaction and bias towards the aging: Attitudes of middle and older adult church members. *Journal of Religious Gerontology, 8,* 59-72.

Sobsey, D., & Doe, T. (1991). Patterns of sexual abuse and assault. *Journal of Sexuality and Disability, 9,* 243-259.

Tattara, T. (1998). *Attitudes toward elder mistreatment and reporting: A multicultural study* (Interim Report). Washington, DC: National Center on Elder Abuse.

Thomas, C. (2000). The first national study of elder abuse and neglect: Contrast with results from other studies. *Journal of Elder Abuse and Neglect, 12*(1), 1.

Twomey, M. (2004). In focus: Faith-based outreach, honoring thy father and thy mother: Reaching the faith community for elder abuse prevention. *National Center on Elder Abuse Newsletter, 6*(5), 2-3.

Underwood, R. (1991). The aging of the church and the teaching of pastoral care. *Journal of Religious Gerontology, 8*(1), 1-11.

Wicks, D. (1996). A minister's information-handling: Protections and constraints on a pastor's care giving. *Journal of Religious and Theological Information, 2*(2), 29-48.

Wolf, R. (1992). Victimization of the elderly: Elder abuse and neglect. *Reviews in Clinical Gerontology, 2*(3), 269-276.

Youngman, B. (1989). Professional and lay religious leaders beliefs and knowledge about older people: A short report. *Journal of Religion and Aging, 5*(1/2), 93-99.

Zborowsky, E. (1985). Developments in protective services: A challenge for social workers. *Journal of Gerontological Social Work, 8*(3/4), 71-83.

Empowering Spirituality
and Generativity
Through Intergenerational
Connections

Sandy J. Eggers, PhD
Beth H. Hensley, RN, EdD

SUMMARY. Intergenerational programming has received much attention and has been heralded as beneficial for both children and older adults. However, little has been reported in the literature concerning adult reactions to and benefits of intergenerational activities. A report on the first two years of an ongoing intergenerational project involving a preschool and a retirement community is presented. Four adults who participated regularly were interviewed in depth and findings are reported. All categories from the interviews represented aspects of

---

Sandy J. Eggers is Director, Emmanuel United Methodist Kindergarten, 2404 Kirby Road, Memphis, TN 38119 (E-mail: sjeggers@emmanuelmemphis.org). Beth H. Hensley is Associate Professor, Southside Regional Medical Center School of Nursing, 801 South Adams Street, Petersburg, VA 23803 (E-mail: beth_hensley@chs.net).

The authors wish to thank Carol Martindale, Activities Director, and Debbie Goodfellow, Assistant Activities Director, of Kirby Pines Retirement Community; and the Junior and Senior Kindergarten teachers of Emmanuel for their invaluable help and support in conceptualizing and executing the "Grandfriends Project."

[Haworth co-indexing entry note]: "Empowering Spirituality and Generativity Through Intergenerational Connections." Eggers, Sandy J., and Beth H. Hensley. Co-published simultaneously in *Journal of Religion, Spirituality & Aging* (The Haworth Pastoral Press, an imprint of The Haworth Press, Inc.) Vol. 17, No. 1/2, 2004, pp. 87-108; and: *Spiritual Assessment and Intervention with Older Adults: Current Directions and Applications* (ed: Mark Brennan, and Deborah Heiser) The Haworth Pastoral Press, an imprint of The Haworth Press, Inc., 2004, pp. 87-108. Single or multiple copies of this article are available for a fee from The Haworth Document Delivery Service [1-800-HAWORTH, 9:00 a.m. - 5:00 p.m. (EST). E-mail address: docdelivery@haworthpress. com].

Erikson's Generativity stage, and indicated that spirituality was enhanced through intergenerational contacts. Opportunities to interact
with young children engendered a sense of relatedness to others and
hope for the future for the older adult interviewees. Implications of this
program that strengthened links to younger generations, and fostered
positive affect, well-being, and spirituality in the aging process are discussed. *[Article copies available for a fee from The Haworth Document Delivery
Service: 1-800-HAWORTH. E-mail address: <docdelivery@haworthpress.com>
Website: <http://www.HaworthPress.com> © 2004 by The Haworth Press, Inc.
All rights reserved.]*

KEYWORDS. Retirement, Erikson, personal growth

There has been an increased interest in intergenerational connections
in the last twenty-five years (Newman, 1989; Travis, Stremmel, &
Duprey, 1993). Today's age-segregated society is missing important aspects of human development by failing to utilize the talents and wisdom
of older adults, by shielding young children from the realities of aging,
and by disconnecting children from their traditions (Chamberlain,
Fetterman, & Maher, 1994). Many families are separated from grandparents by geographical distances, and many older adults are housed in
assisted living facilities and nursing homes, creating an isolation of age
groups (Newman, Christopher, Smith, Wilson, & McCrea, 1997). Providing programming which purposefully connects the generations offers benefits for both age groups (Iiales, Hiclund, & Hiftin, 2000;
Kaplan, 1993), in that promoting life's purpose and meaning and significant connections with others are long-recognized components of spiritual well-being (Chandler, Holden, & Kolander, 1992; Lindgren &
Coursey, 1995; Pargament, 1997).

There are many obvious benefits to greater contact between younger
and older generations. Children, who have been shown to have negative
perceptions of being old (Haught, Walls, Laney, Leavell, & Stuzen,
1999; Jantz, Seefeldt, Galper, & Serock, 1977; Langer, 1999; Steitz &
Verner, 1987), are afforded an opportunity to connect with older adults
as real people and to better understand the process of aging. Seniors
have a connection to the joys of young children and a perception of being useful which adds purpose and meaning to their existence (Seefeldt,
Jantz, Serock, & Bredekamp, 1982). The intergenerational research literature, however, is dominated by studies that examine children's per-

ceptions of aging and affects of intergenerational programming on these perceptions. The effects that this programming has on older adult lives, including those that may support spiritual well-being, have rarely been examined. The purpose of this article is to evaluate the impact of one intergenerational program, the Grandfriend Project, on the spiritual well-being of older adult participants through qualitative analysis.

Intergenerational Contacts and Personal Development

According to Erik Erikson (1980), the major tasks of adulthood are Generativity and, in the later years, to maintain a sense of Integrity in the face of multiple losses. Erik Erikson defines Generativity as being interested in the foundation and guidance of future generations, whether they are one's biological offspring or not. All definitions of Generativity involve perceiving one's self as connected with a future that will survive and continue after one is gone, giving of self to the future, and a hope that the future is secure (McFadden, 1985; Rubenstein, 1988). In *The Life Cycle Completed* (1997) Joan Erikson stated, "Integrity has the function of promoting contact with the world, with things, and above all, with people" (p. 8).

Our society is growing older as people are living longer and young adults are having fewer children; the fastest growing age group is the oldest old (U.S. Census Bureau, 2000a, 2000b). With the older adult population growing at such a fast pace, it is increasingly important to maintain quality of life in the later years. It has been assumed that intergenerational programming is beneficial for both populations involved (Newman, Christopher, Smith, Wilson, & McCrea, 1997).

The Impact of Intergenerational Programs on Older Adults

Because there is little formal research literature that has measured adult reactions to involvement with young children (Lambert, Dellman-Jenkins, & Fruit, 1990; Stremmel, Travis, Kelly-Harrison, & Hensley, 1994), little support exists for the positive impact of intergenerational contacts for older adults. However, there is limited support for the notion that intergenerational programs have positive effects on the lives of older people. For example, Dellman-Jenkins (1997) found that older adults had a heightened sense of well-being when they perceived that children found them fun to be around. Larkin and Newman (2001) reported that older adult volunteers in childcare settings perceived that they were able to be a good role model for healthy aging and that their lives were enriched by the laughter, hugs and the sense of being needed. Pinquart, Wenzel and Sorensen (2000) found that intergenerational programming improved older adult attitudes toward children, but that older adult self-concept was unaffected. The Intergeneration Innovations Web page (http://www.intergenerate.org) states that intergenerational programs, ". . . reduce isolation, boost self-esteem, reinforce that they [older adults] are needed by the community, stimulate mental capacity, promote life-long learning, reconnect them [older adults] with their community, introduce them [older adults] to new experiences with children from diverse background, and rekindle the joy of living." While all of this may be true, there needs to be empirical evidence involving a systematic evaluation of older adult reactions to involvement with children, and assessment and definition of the impact that children may have on older adult lives.

The Grandfriend Project

The Grandfriend Project intergenerational program was implemented with the goal of providing meaningful relationships between preschool children and older adults that would foster understanding of the aging process for the children, as well as promote spiritual well-being for the older adult participants by adding purpose and meaning to life and promoting the spiritual joy of meaningful connections with children through opportunities for expressions of Generativity. A unique aspect of the Grandfriend Project is that it has been ongoing for two years, and is now beginning the third year. Some older adults have had an opportunity to form strong relationships with the children, with teachers, and with other school personnel. These meaningful relationships enhance the sense of spirituality for the older adults through a sense of connectedness with the children and hope in the future generation. An overview of how this intergenerational intervention was implemented is presented below.

Year One (2001-2002). The older adult participants in the Grandfriends Project were residents of Kirby Pines Retirement Community and lived in the independent living section of this community. The child participants were enrolled at Emmanuel United Methodist Kindergarten. Emmanuel Kindergarten is a private, faith-based preschool in an upper-middle-class neighborhood in Memphis, Tennessee. Kirby Pines is two miles from the kindergarten, and many residents of Kirby Pines attend Emmanuel United Methodist Church. Thus, the connection between these two institutions was a natural one, and the older adult and child populations were a good match. In the summer of 2001 the Activities Director of Kirby Pines and the Director of Emmanuel Kindergarten met to plan an ongoing program for children and adults to interact with one another at both sites.

It was decided to solicit adult participation, and then pair the children with the older adults. Each older adult "Grandfriend" ($n = 23$) was paired with two children from two classes at Emmanuel ($n = 56$) consisting of 30 girls and 26 boys from 4 to 6-years-old. A variety of activities were provided over the course of the school year, with the goal of offering multiple opportunities to communicate and work together. According to Seefeldt (1987) who applied the "Contact Hypothesis" to intergeneration planning of activities, positive attitudes between the groups are affected by many conditions. Namely, the contacts should be intimate rather than casual, should be pleasant and rewarding for both groups and should be functional. These goals guided the planning for the intergenerational programming. Activities were held at both the school and the retirement community so that the children could understand the adults' world and the adults could see the children in their environments. This "layering" of activities provided a basis for communication for the children and adults and promoted getting to know one another well; significant emotional bonds formed between many of the older adults and children. These interactions between the older adults and the children helped cultivate spiritual well-being by providing opportunities for connectedness with others and adding a sense of purpose to the lives of the older adults.

The first three activities were designed to offer opportunities for the older adults and children to complete arts and crafts projects, engage in games, have snacks, and participate in programs together. In October 2001 the children went to Kirby Pines for a "Fall Festival." The children were first introduced to their special "Grandfriends," and then played many games such as beanbag toss, go fishing, and pin the tail on the donkey. Each older adult assisted their assigned children in all activities. There were additional opportunities for social interaction when the adults and children had snacks together.

The second gathering brought the adults to Emmanuel in November. The children and adults took Polaroid pictures, decorated frames for the pictures, made a snack, and acted out the Thanksgiving Day story together. The children also took their Grandfriend to visit their classroom. In December, the children went back to Kirby Pines, taking with them snowmen they had made for Kirby Pines to use for Christmas decorations. Santa visited and the children sang Christmas songs for the residents. All shared a snack together.

Following these three events, the two directors assessed what had been done so far, and decided to continue the project by providing more opportunities for individual contacts. By this time several older adults ($n = 6$) had decided to no longer participate because of conflicting schedules or because they found it difficult to be with the children. Some of the latter had physical constraints, which hindered them from feeling comfortable around such active children, although the children were well behaved in general. Enthusiastic older adult participants in the project recruited four other residents so that only four children had to be rematched.

The adult Grandfriends signed up for times in January 2002 to come visit in the classroom with their children. They spent about two hours interacting with the children and participating in daily class activities. In February and March, the children visited Kirby Pines. At each visit, from two to four adult Grandfriends and their Emmanuel children, accompanied by some parents and the school director, met in the snack bar at Kirby Pines. Here they had a snack together, and then toured the retirement facility and visited the apartments of their Grandfriend. Most of the older adults shared their hobbies and special interests with the children as they visited. The Grandfriends also took special pride in showing the children where they had displayed pictures from the November event. Upon returning to the school, the children shared their experiences through drawing and story writing.

The year was concluded with a picnic on the grounds at Kirby Pines. The children and older adults blew bubbles, tried to hula-hoop, played whiffle ball, fished, etc. Lastly, the older adults came to Emmanuel's year-end sing-a-long where they watched the children sing and met the parents of their special children if they had not already met them at previous events.

Year Two (2002-2003). Some changes to the Grandfriends Project were made in the second year. For example, many disappointments occurred in the first year when an older adult dropped out of the program, or when a child was sick, etc. Thus, it was decided that the program would include only one class of kindergarten children ($n = 36$; 20 girls and 16 boys), and that the adults and children would not be paired except for those children who were returning to Emmanuel and who already had a special Grandfriend. This idea worked well, as the children and older adults seemed to be drawn to someone with whom they had shared activities in the past, but were not devastated if their special friend was not present for an event.

Additionally, many lessons were learned the second year as Kirby Pines had a series of changes in activities directors. However, the older adult participants were very committed to the program and would not let it die. The Assistant Activities Director eventually took charge of the program since so many Grandfriends persisted in their desire to have contact with the children. The children went to Kirby Pines twice for games, songs, dancing, and lunch. The adults came to Emmanuel Kindergarten for Christmas sing-a-longs, for a day of Bingo and decorating cookies, and for the children's "graduation" from Emmanuel. Following the graduation the older adults and families of the children visited with each other and had refreshments. At this point in the program several of the children had been with the same adult for two years, but the children were going to be in other schools the following year. There were some tearful goodbyes and some very touching moments at this gathering. The program is now planning for the third year.

Purpose and Rationale

Anecdotal evidence, as well as the strong commitment on the part of older adult participants to continue the Grandfriends Project in the second year, provides support for the continuation of this intervention as a means of strengthening intergenerational connections between older adults and children. Following the second year of the project, four older adult participants provided in-depth interviews of their experiences with the project. The purpose of this article is to systematically evaluate the impact of the Grandfriend Project on the spiritual well-being of older adult participants through qualitative analysis based on these four interviews.

METHOD

Sample

After two years of participation in the Grandfriends Project, four of the older adults were interviewed about their interactions with the children. These adults were chosen because they had had a two-year relationships with the children with whom they were initially paired, and because they had expressed enthusiasm about the program. All four of them had shared very special experiences with the children from Emmanuel Kindergarten. Two other adults were asked to participate in interviews and agreed to do so, but their busy schedules never allowed time to complete the interview. Interviews were conducted in the residences of the older adults.

Measures

A questionnaire was devised to direct semi-structured interviews with the four older adult Grandfriends who participated. The interview questions were designed to encourage the adults to share both their positive and negative experiences with the children, their feelings about being with the children, opinions about older adult participation in the project, and things that could be done to enhance the program. A copy of this questionnaire is provided in the Appendix.

In addition, over the course of the two years of the Grandfriends Project, the Director of Emmanuel Kindergarten kept a record of specific stories and anecdotes that occurred as a result of the contact between the children and the older adults. The interviews and anecdotes from the two years of interactions were used to evaluate the impact of intergenerational programming on the lives of these older individuals and were used as qualitative data in the present analyses.

Procedures

The Director of Emmanuel Kindergarten and an additional researcher who had been present at most activities conducted the interviews. The older adults were comfortable with this arrangement since they had interacted with both individuals throughout the project. Informed consent was obtained, and the Directors of Kirby Pines granted permission for the interviews to take place on site. The interviews lasted approximately 90 minutes, and were recorded and later transcribed. Many conversations strayed from the Grandfriend experiences per se, as the older adults enjoyed sharing personal experiences with children and their own childhood experiences from the past.

Qualitative Analysis

Verbatim responses were recorded in order to capture the essence of what the older adults had to share, and were subjected to qualitative content analysis. From these transcripts, a "Grounded Theory" approach was used with categories of responses developed post facto based on the actual words from the interview responses (Glaser & Strauss, 1967). That is, no attempt was made to code the data using categories in advance. The first step in the coding process was to conduct repeated readings of the transcriptions to gain a sense of the essential meanings and key themes posed for each question (Taylor & Bogdan, 1984). Two judges independently generated coding categories for the responses, and then evaluated for the categories for similarity and overlap. Any discrepancies were discussed until consensus was reached.

RESULTS

Several themes emerged from the interviews and anecdotes that demonstrate what these contacts have meant to the older adults who have participated in the Grandfriends Project. Overall, these themes show how this intervention addressed spiritual well-being by providing opportunities for older adults to express generative concerns, which in turn fostered a sense of life's purpose and meaning and significant connections to others. The themes have been labeled below and are followed with supporting example quotes and anecdotes.

Expressions of Generativity

The Grandfriends Project was aimed at establishing connections between younger and older generations, which forms the essence of generative concerns (Erikson, 1980). The importance of having opportunities to express Generativity was evident in a number of themes that emerged from qualitative analysis.

Joyfulness and Fun in Being Together. All adults were very animated and full of laughter as they recalled events with the children. It is clear that simply being around the children brought much joy into their lives. For example, after spending the morning at Emmanuel with his two children, one of the Grandfriends remarked, "These boys just give me such a charge. I didn't feel too good today, but now I'm fine. They made me laugh and play. We had so much fun." Another participant remarked on how the project enabled relationships that would not have been possible without the intervention, "I enjoy it, I enjoy the children and I never had children of my own, but I've always loved children." Many respondents talked about how they were pleased with the nature of interactions with young children. For example, one said, "I look forward to seeing the kids, seeing the expressions on their faces–lots of laughter–that's fun to me. They don't let anything bother them." Another told us, "When they came over here and we did those things on the dance floor–whoa they got with it! I tell you that Macarena and all that was something, and us trying to do it with them amused the children." One participant noted how even those older adults who chose not to participate enjoyed the presence of the children in their community, "But I think that when the people over here that aren't even involved in this program, they will stop and watch like they [the children] are just wonders, and they are. It gives all of us a joy." Another said, "Those two boys I had last year, they were just so nice to me. You know, when you get to our age, you appreciate children more. I think we're all that way."

Other examples of how this intergenerational program injected joy into the lives of its older adult participants were:

> If I had to choose one favorite thing–going to the classroom and spending time with the children. We played a guessing game–that was real cute, being with the children in their environment. That was one of the highlights–seeing them doing their thing. She was over there cooking, just being as busy as she could be and then they had this little bed over there. She was just acting like a little lady. Then of course when we went in this little room, they sat in their places. Then there was this little boy pretending to be a puppy dog. They were just so funny and cute. I still laugh about that day. It's just little things like that I think are fabulous.

> I have another thing I believe in very strongly. No one will remember what you said and very likely won't remember what you did, but will remember how you made them feel when you were associated with them. When I come over there to see you all I feel VERY good. I enjoy it; I really do, just because I enjoy you [the interviewer] and the children.

Faith That the Future Is Secure in the Next Generation. Another important component of Generativity is that there is continuity and a secure future for future generations. This was clearly a concern for the older adults at Kirby Pines, as the Activities Director observed that some older adults did not want to participate in the Grandfriends project because they thought that the children of today are ill behaved and mean, and they had written off the younger generation. However, the older adults who were interviewed found it refreshing that the children actually knew how to behave. For example, in terms of the children's behavior, one person told us, "I guess I'm a disciplinarian. I like to see children behave. I like that about your program." Another told us, "I like the picnic that we had. They were so nice at that picnic, E. and P. both; and they sat down and we ate together; and all the bubble blowing and all was just great and the kids were SO well behaved." And one said, "I particularly like the after-church program that you had and they [the children] were so good in the church." Other remarks that supported this theme included: "They're precious and they are the future of our country"; and "I've seen children be around older people and they'd shy away and not even talk to them. And somebody young they talk to, but not older people. I see these children talk to older people and it really does me good. It really does."

Older adults were also reassured that the adults working with the children still had standards that met the expectations of their generation, giving them a sense of hope for the future. One Grandfriend told us, "You all have made us feel great–to see you interested in children makes me feel so good." Other remarks that addressed this theme included:

> Another thing that I like about the program is the parents, how they really join in, it seems like, and you have things so under control. And you say, come on over here and they will. I think that all of you over there, including you, is how you handle the children, it's a piece of work, I tell you.

> They are younger than our grandchildren are. Seeing the children over there and being close to them has made me appreciate the education and what the children are doing these days. I talk to some people that are ready to write off children as being mean. . . . It makes you feel really good when you are around a group that you know is not that way and not gonna be that way. It makes me feel a lot better about the future.

Life's Purpose and Meaning Through Helping the Younger Generation

One of the major components of spirituality, as described above, is having a sense that life is both purposeful and meaningful (Chandler et al., 1992; Lindgren & Coursey, 1995). One of the themes to emerge from the interviews with Grandfriend participants was how the opportunities for generative expression enhanced their sense of purpose and meaning in life. For example, M., an older woman participant, is an accomplished artist. She painted a small picture for each of her children after spending time with them for a year. When asked about doing the paintings she said, "Well I just wanted to give them something. I thought, well they have all these toys and material things, but they don't have their own personal painting. So I just did a hummingbird for them. They seemed to appreciate it." Another older man shared his love of music with the children:

> I played my guitar a little bit, and my fiddle a little bit [when the children visited his apartment]. I play a fiddle, not a violin. I like to play for young folks. They are not too demanding in that respect because they haven't studied music yet. They'll catch ya–they're

sharp, they're sharp. . . . We hadn't planned to do that [play music] when they came up here. They saw the guitar in the closet and right off wanted to know what it was. It was sort of spontaneous. I said, "I'll just show you how I play." And I did, and they seemed to really enjoy that. And–uh–I would–as you know they say–any child is poor without musical training and I believe that. It's meant a lot to me over the years.

Others felt their participation instilled purpose in their lives because it gave them the opportunity to guide the younger generation. One person said, "I think the saddest children in the world are those that don't have anybody that care if they live or die, and it's surprising how many there are like that." Another remarked, "I feel like you can make a difference by caring for these children." Still another resident said, "They are so sweet and so innocent and now is the time that they are to be molded for their future and I just believe that we ought to do that." One participant felt that the opportunity to interact with young children could provide guidance at an important juncture in their lives, "I'm a firm believer in the saying that everything I need to know I learned in Kindergarten. It's built upon throughout life. They get the snips out of it all along as they go." Still another attributed her participation due to the opportunity to help children, "Do you think it helps the children? Me-that's one of the main reasons I'm doing it. That's what my daughter says about my grandchildren coming here. They've made some real friends here." One person spelled this out during the interview:

I know that children now days think different than we did when we were growing up, don't you think? I don't think children are growing up as courteous as we did when we grew up. We were taught to say "yes Ma'am" and "no Ma'am" and now it's "What?!" "What do you want?" and things like that. That's the difference I see in the younger generation. I know there's a lot of them that are raised different. The parents are different, I really think that. We were just taught different. We were taught to respect our elders and I don't think that children really do that any more. Do you know what I'm saying? That bothers me. I like to think these children will be different.

Other Grandfriends thought that their participation in the project would help the children to better understand aging and older people. As one person said, "I think it will give the children good tolerance for older people that I think some people don't have-and too some older people don't have tolerance for children." Another related, "And if there is anything you can say and do to be an encouragement to a child . . . you know a lot of children don't get that ever. You know that." One person told the interviewer:

> I enjoy just being with them, and I'll tell you the truth we are not exposed to the intergenerational gap very much, and I think it makes them [the children] realize one of these days I'll be getting old. I think it gives them a better picture of the total of life because young people today think they are going to live forever and they're just not.

Feeling Wanted and Needed. Purpose and meaning were also engendered in older participants by feeling wanted and needed by the children who participated in the project. To illustrate, at kindergarten graduation, one six-year-old looked at his Grandfriend and said to her, "It's been the best two years of my life being with you." One child, C., who is being raised by his grandparents, said to his Grandfriend Ms. B. when he first met her two years ago: "Now I finally have a grandmother!" For the next two years, C. told everyone that Ms. B. was his grandmother. Both C. and Ms. B. are members of Emmanuel church and saw each other on Sundays. C. learned that his Grandfriend and her husband almost always parked in the same place on Sunday mornings. Thereafter he would meet them and help them into church by holding the door for them, etc.

In another instance, N. went to Kirby Pines and his Grandfriend could not attend the function because she was sick. N. went back to school and wrote her a letter that contained the following: "I would like to know what you would like to do the next time I see you. I missed you. I like you very much. You are my special friend." Because young children are honest and unassuming, it was very gratifying to the older adults to realize that they were special to these children, and that the children would miss them if they were not there, and that the children need them. As one respondent put it, "They are so non-assuming. They don't expect anything and if you do anything for them, they appreciate it." Participants also felt wanted and needed because of the enthusiasm the children expressed toward being with their Grandfriend. One older person related a story about going into the classroom and her child being so excited to see her that she tried to climb over another child to get to her, "G. was just struggling to get to ME. I just reached over and just lifted her up. Things like that just tickle me to death. Those are wonderful memories." Another remarked: .

> The way that the kids when they see us, they run to us. It's just that old thing about human nature that the older you get the more you like children, cause you're more like them I guess. It's a great experience.

Significant Connections with Others

As noted previously, vital connections with others are one of the components of spirituality and well-being (Chandler et al., 1992; Lindgren & Coursey, 1995; Pargament, 1997). Analysis of the Grandfriends Project revealed how opportunities to express Generativity also helped to forge these important relationships. For example, one of the many Grandfriends who had no grandchildren was surprised by a visit from one of her Emmanuel children on Mother's Day. The child's mother just decided to go by Kirby Pines that day and see if they could find her and give her a hug. Kirby Pines had a fishing rodeo, a picnic and other special activities for families that day. Miss M. was enjoying watching others and participating in whatever she could when the child and his mother came. This child and his mother stayed all afternoon, and the boy loved all the events and even won the fishing rodeo. This Grandfriend told the interviewers that she had the best Mother's Day she had ever had.

In another instance, during the first year of the project when the children and older adults got together at Christmas one of the older adults had a very special gift to give her child. This adult never had had a little girl; all of her children and grandchildren had been boys. She spent considerable time shopping for the perfect doll that looked like her little child who was a girl. She said, "I never got to buy a doll for my children, and I wanted to get the perfect doll for J."

The importance of these intergenerational connections was revealed by other statements about the positive interactions that took place as part of the project. One Grandfriend said, "The most meaningful thing is just being with the children and interacting with them. All these other things they just fall into place if you can do that and just open your heart and your mind." Another told the interviewers in reference to her younger friends, "G. is the sweetest little thing, I just love her and could hug her to death. It's the same way with J." Another resident spoke to the power of the bond with these children relative to other activities in the retirement community, "That connection that you make with the children, you can have all the programs to do, but your bonding with your little friend, to me is IT." Others saw this project as filling an important gap in the social networks of these older adults, "Some of these people here don't have grandchildren then this is important for them. This fills a nice place for them. S. only has one granddaughter and doesn't have a lot of contact with her."

Creating Memories and Bonds That Continued to Bring Joy. The contact between Grandfriends and the children was responsible for creating joyful memories and bonds that evidenced the importance of these intergenerational connections. When going to Kirby Pines to see his Grandfriend's room, N. decided to take her a piece of his birthday cake. The cake was all flat and "squished" by the time it got to Kirby Pines, but he gave it to Ms. S. anyway. Ms. S. was thrilled and has mentioned that piece of birthday cake and laughed about it every time the school director has seen her since that time.

K., a six-year-old, is the son of a music minister at Emmanuel. K. goes with his father to Kirby Pines when he leads worship and enjoys visiting with his Grandfriend from a year ago. As one resident related, "They [her two children] came out and spent an hour with me a couple of times. That was nice. They invited me to Thanksgiving dinner, but I didn't go." Another said, "You can form lifelong bonds with these children if you so desire. And I just think it's a wonderful program." The spiritual nature of these connections was revealed by one resident who said, "I think the particular life long blessing that we'll have are the life long memories that we'll have of these children and the people that are over there taking care of them. They say you are a part of everyone you met. I believe that." One participant shared the following story:

> The one I think was the cutest was A. came running up to me and said "Where's your wheel chair?" He'd been told obviously that he was coming to a retirement home. Well I don't have one yet. "Well, when you gonna get one?" I told him I hope not for a long time. He just couldn't believe that I didn't have a wheel chair.

The Activities Director of Kirby Pines reported that the older adults often shared special memories of being with the children. Almost every time a Grandfriend caught the school Director informally, something that was special to them about the children was related and brought laughter. When visiting the Grandfriends' apartments, it was noticed that most of them had pictures of the children and artwork by the children displayed somewhere in their apartment. These mementos brought pleasure and kept the connections alive.

Older Adult Reactions to the Intervention

As the preceding comments illustrate, older adult Grandfriends were very enthusiastic about the opportunity to participate in this intervention. Although a small number ($n = 6$) dropped out after the first year, often because of poor health, the majority of participants wanted to continue a second year and helped to recruit other older adults to replace the drop-outs. One of the measures of success of this program was evidenced by a desire of these older adults to encourage others to participate-helping their generation understand the importance of connecting with young children.

Increasing Participation. All of the older adults interviewed were concerned about getting more of the adults at Kirby Pines involved in the program. One was bothered about an apparent gender bias among the older Grandfriends, "We need to get more men involved." Other participants noted other barriers: "I'd like to see more people around here involved in this program. They have lots of excuses and reasons." The compassion of the older adults for the children, being with them, and the sense of joy in doing so made them eager to find ways to convince others to share in these experiences. As one person put it, "I've enjoyed this one so much and I don't understand why more people don't volunteer," and another said, "I tell others that we need to be there for these children."

Others talked about how older adults would benefit from being participants in the Grandfriends Project. One said, "I just think it's a great program and we interact with the children and it would mean a whole lot in anyone's life to interact with these children because they just bring so much pleasure into your life." Another related, "I just think it's a wonderful program and it's meant a lot to me. I can't imagine not doing it." One older Grandfriend had an ideal of having a very large group of adults participating:

> I'd like to have a group of about 50 [adults] then if 40 of them have "hair fixin' day" that day there would still be some. Now we just have to kind of do it [the activities] with who comes, and sometimes we don't have enough [adults] to do with all the children.

Grandfriends and Opportunities for Personal Growth. The respondents who were interviewed after the second year of the project noted that their participation also provided opportunities for continued growth and development on their part. One avenue for such growth was that they continued to learn and have challenges due to their interaction with the younger children. As one older Grandfriend put it, "You see their little minds just a working, you know, and they are just a learning. Have you ever thought of it that way? You just see their minds working and taking it in." Another older adult told the interviewer, "I look forward to getting with the children because you can learn a lot from these children. It's amazing what those little minds have up there, it really is!" Some felt that appreciating the differences amongst the children was an important plus to the program: "I like to watch them and the difference in the children and the things that they do. That means a lot." Another said, "I was really interested in the autistic child that you had. I watched her a lot." Still another felt that the project provided opportunities for the participants to foster a sense of love and compassion toward the younger generation: "Everyone that I know of that has participated in it has more love for children and more tolerance for children." Two participants noted the rejuvenating effects of interacting with young children. One said, "Any time that you are older and associated with children, I believe that it makes you feel younger. They make you get up and move around some. It is a wonderful thing." Another related:

> When you interact with young people you stay younger longer and that's a fact. It really is (laugh). I think laughing is the best medicine there is, I really do. This program has just enhanced my life here, it really has. It's something I look forward to. They are precious; they are just precious souls.

DISCUSSION

The adults involved in the Grandfriends Project were connected with the younger generation in a very concrete way. They perceived themselves as offering guidance to the future. They have hope that the children and adults who work with them will continue to guide the world. Additionally, their participation helped them to realize that they as older adults have an opportunity to participate in contributing this gift to the world. Connections with the children, memories and joy experienced in being with them, and a sense of being helpful promoted integrity in their lives as they faced the realities of growing older. These adults were in the developmental process of integrating the past, present and future, as well as transcending the limitations of the self through these intergenerational links (Erikson, 1997). Spiritual well-being is supported as one finds a sense of meaning and purpose for one's existence and establishes vital connections to others in this process.

A sense of purpose in existence and presence in life is a driving force for well-being. It is both intuitive and a well-documented fact that this sense of purpose is more elusive in later life (Levin, 1994). In Western society one's identity, purpose and well-being are closely tied with independence and life work. When one's career is over and one can no longer live independently, living a purposeful life becomes a challenging task. It is clear that the older adults who participated in the Grandfriends Project have realized that the connection to young children has given them a purpose and meaning for existence. These older adults have responsibilities to the children for encouraging them, teaching them, and being present in order for them to learn about growing old. Participants also sensed an urgency to encourage their older adult peers to understand what they do, namely, that the lives of these children are important and that their own personal well-being as well as the future well-being of society depends on being involved with the younger generations.

Maintaining a sense of Integrity in the face of losing one's physical capacities, losing purpose as work identity is gone, and losing the companionship of departed loved ones and friends is very difficult (J. Erikson, 1997). The adult Grandfriends involved in this intergenerational project have found a new joy and pleasure in their lives. They feel needed by the children and have gained relationships that give them a sense of purpose and a joy as they anticipate more encounters with the children. At the end of each activity, the Grandfriends inquire about future get-togethers. For a little while they feel younger and they know that they have learned something new by being with the children. They have grown, they have contributed to the well-being of others and society, and they have joy and memories to brighten their days even as they face the end of life. Thus, in the face of despair, these older adults have opportunities to feel good about themselves and the future, and strengthen their sense of Integrity.

Definitions of spirituality include the concepts of inner-connectedness, an ability to transcend immediate circumstances, and a sense of meaning and purpose in life (Chandler et al., 1992; Lindgren & Coursey, 1995; Pargament, 1997). Connecting with the children allowed the adults to find additional meaning by contributing knowledge about life to the younger generation, and by helping them in their daily activities. The joyful times together promoted transcendence over the daily concerns of growing older, and the fond memories sustained this transcendence. As the adults bonded with the children their sense of connectedness with life across its entire span became illuminated, and a sense of hope in the future was generated. Thus, many aspects of spirituality, by definition, were enhanced when older adults had the opportunity to experience meaningful relationships between the generations.

The older adults in this study experienced a sense of oneness with all ages. They were compassionate about the children, but were also concerned for their peers who do not understand the value of being with the children. This caring concern for all shows a desire to use hope, which resides in Integrity, to activate hope in others (McFadden, 1985). The older Grandfriends have a commitment to continue to grow and they have a relatedness to others that according to Erikson (1980) is generative love. This generative love supports spiritual growth as one creates a kind of immortality through the connectedness and hope for the future. The trust and hope achieved in reaching out to younger generations can become a legacy for the older adult. Spiritual maturity cannot be attained without relational interdependence (Moberg, 1990).

There is much to be learned from these older adults who find such meaning in investing time with children. Today's world has what has been called a "discontinuity of family life." With older adults separated from family by geographical location and by living arrangements (Cantor & Brennan, 2000), it is more difficult to attain the "grand-generative function," the function of Generativity with one's grandchildren and children of future generations (Erikson, 1997). Opportunities for older adults to act upon their commitment to the future are limited by the context of their lives (McFadden, 1985). These adults in the Grandfriends Project have seized a chance to be actively involved and connected. From these older individuals we can learn how it is possible to continue to have a sense of purpose and maintain the connectedness that is so vital to spiritual well-being. They have a commitment to the future and are fulfilling new roles that enable them to act upon that commitment.

Limitations of this project exist in the case study approach used for evaluation. This article represents one school's experience with intergenerational programming and its associated benefits. Thus, the generalizability of the findings to the older adult population as a whole and to other programs remains to be examined. However, it is clear that the older adults who participated in this project gained valuable experiences, had increased quality of life, and opportunities for spiritual growth from the intergenerational connections. The program was voluntary, so only adults who were interested in children participated. Reaching all older adults through this kind of programming is not actually feasible because many older adults do not feel comfortable relating to a child's world. It is interesting, however, that several of the adults who had few life opportunities to be with children still participated in the project and enjoyed interacting with the children.

As mentioned above, the program has been affected by frequent changes in activity directors at the retirement community. Consistency in leadership and commitment to intergenerational programming would be beneficial to the success of this program. The program is unique in the kinds of activities provided and the sustained intergenerational connections. Although this paper has focused on the older adults, all who participated in this program benefited from their involvement, including the directors, teachers, the children, and the parents. The success experienced indicates that the Grandfriends Project could be a model for other religious communities (e.g., churches, synagogues), schools, and retirement facilities.

REFERENCES

Cantor, M. H., & Brennan, M. (2000). *Social care of the elderly: The effects of ethnicity, class, and culture.* New York: Springer.

Chamberlain, V., Fetterman, E., & Mahler, M. (1994). Innovation in elder and child care: An intergenerational experience. *Educational Gerontology, 19,* 193-205.

Chandler, C. K., Holden, J. M., & Kolander, C. A. (1992). Counseling for spiritual wellness: Theory and practice. *Journal of Counseling & Development, 71,* 168-174.

Dellman-Jenkins, M. (1997). A senior-centered model of intergenerational programming with young children. *The Journal of Applied Gerontology, 16,* 495-505.

Erickson, E. (1980). *Identity and the life cycle.* New York: W.W. Norton & Company.

Erickson, J. (1997). *The life cycle completed.* New York: W.W. Norton & Company.

Glaser, B., & Strauss, A. (1967). *The discovery of grounded theory.* Chicago: Aldine.

Haught, P., Walls, R., Laney, J., Leavell, A., & Stuzen, S. (1999). Child and adolescent knowledge and attitudes about older adults across time and states. *Educational Gerontology, 25,* 501-517.

Iiales, S., Hiclund, S., & Hiflin, C. (2000). Children's perceptions of elders before and after a school-based intergenerational program. *Educational Gerontology, 26,* 677-688.

Jantz, R., Seefeldt, C., Galper, A., & Serock, K. (1977). Children's attitudes toward the elderly. *Social Education, 41,* 518-523.

Kaplan, M. (1993). Recruiting senior adult volunteers for intergenerational programs: Working to create a "Jump on the Bandwagon" effect. *The Journal of Applied Gerontology, 12,* 71-90.

Lambert, D., Dellman-Jenkins, M., & Fruit, D. (1990). Planning for contact between the generations: An effective approach. *The Gerontologist, 30*, 85-89.

Langer, N. (1999). Changing youngsters' perceptions of aging: Aging education's role. *Educational Gerontology, 25* (6), 549-554.

Larkin, E., & Newman, S. (2001). Benefits of intergenerational staffing in preschools. *Educational Gerontology, 27*, 372-385.

Levin, J. (1994). Investigation of the epidemiologic effects of religious experience: Findings, explanations, barriers. In J. S. Levin (Ed.), *Religion in aging and health: Theoretical foundations and methodological frontiers* (pp. 3-17). Thousand Oakes, CA: Sage Publications.

Lindgren, K. N., & Coursey, R. D. (1995). Spirituality and serious mental illness: A two-part study. *Psychosocial Rehabilitation Journal, 18*, 93-107.

McFadden, S. (1985). Attributes of religious maturity in aging people. *Journal of Religion and Aging, 1*(3), 39-48.

Moberg, D. (1990). Spiritual maturity and wholeness in the later years. *Journal of Religious Gerontology, 7*(1), 5-24.

Newman, S. (1989). A history of intergenerational programs. *Journal of Children in Contemporary Society, 20*(3-4), 1-16.

Newman, S., Christopher, R., Smith, T., Wilson, J., and McCrea, J. (1997). *Intergenerational programs: Past, present and future.* Washington, DC: Taylor & Francis Publishing.

Pargament, K. I. (1997). *The psychology of religion and coping.* New York: Guilford Press.

Pinquart, M., Wenzel, S., & Sorensen, S. (2000). Changes in attitudes among children and elderly adults in intergenerational group work. *Educational Gerontology, 28*, 624-640.

Rubinstein, R. (1994). Generativity as pragmatic spirituality. In L. Thomas, & S. Eisenhandler (Eds.), *Aging and the religious dimension* (pp. 169-181). Westport, CT: Auburn House.

Seefeldt, C. (1987). The effects of preschoolers' visits to a nursing home. *The Gerontologist, 27*, 228-232.

Seefeldt, C., Jantz, R., Serock, K., & Bredekamp, S. (1982). Elderly persons' attitudes toward children. *Educational Gerontology, 8*, 493-506.

Steitz, J., & Verner, B. (1987). What adolescents know about aging. *Educational Gerontology, 13*, 357-368.

Stremmel, A., Travis, S., Kelly-Harrison, P., & Hensley, D. (1994). The perceived benefits and problems associated with intergenerational exchanges in day care settings. *The Gerontologist, 34*, 503-519.

Taylor, S. J., & Bogdan, R. (1984). *Qualitative research methods: The search for meanings.* New York: Wiley.

Travis, S., Stremmel, A., & Duprey, P. (1993). Child and adult day care professions converging in 1992: Implications for training and research. *Educational Gerontology, 19*, 285-295.

APPENDIX

Questions for the semi-structured interview with older participants in the Grandfriends Project:

1. Please tell us what the "Grandfriends Project" experience was like for you. What were your feelings about the program?
2. What did you like most about the "Grandfriends Project"? Why?
3. What did you like least about the project? Why?
4. What was meaningful for you about the project?
5. What kind of difference did this experience make for you?
6. What were your feelings about the younger generations before you participated in this program? Have these changed? How?
7. What were your attitudes or ideas about yourself, especially as an older person before participating in this program? Have these changed? How?
8. What kinds of things would you like to see changed about the "Grandfriends" Project this year? Why?
9. Are you continuing with the program next year? Could you please explain what went into your decision?
10. If there was only one thing that you'd like people to know about the "Grandfriends" program, what would that be?

Spiritual Activities for Adults with Alzheimer's Disease: The Cognitive Components of Dementia and Religion

David E. Vance, PhD, MGS

SUMMARY. Engaging adults with Alzheimer's disease in activities can prevent disease related agitation. Finding meaningful and enjoyable activities proves to be a difficult task due to severe damage to explicit memory and executive functioning. Fortunately, many spiritual and religious activities rely on more resilient cognitive features such as procedural memory and limbic system aspects of attachment and motivation. Such spiritual activities, if properly selected, can be used to engage adults with dementia. This approach, called Procedural and Emotional Religious Activity Therapy, can be used by various religious traditions and extended to multiple therapeutic venues. *[Article copies available for a fee from The Haworth Document Delivery Service: 1-800-HAWORTH. E-mail address: <docdelivery@haworthpress.com> Website: <http://www.Haworth Press.com> © 2004 by The Haworth Press, Inc. All rights reserved.]*

David E. Vance is a NIH/NIA Postdoctoral Fellow, Edward R. Roybal Center for Research in Applied Gerontology, The University of Alabama at Birmingham, 924 19th Street South, Suite 110, Birmingham, AL 35294-2100 (E-mail: devance@uab.edu).

[Haworth co-indexing entry note]: "Spiritual Activities for Adults with Alzheimer's Disease: The Cognitive Components of Dementia and Religion." Vance, David E. Co-published simultaneously in *Journal of Religion, Spirituality & Aging* (The Haworth Pastoral Press, an imprint of The Haworth Press, Inc.) Vol. 17, No. 1/2, 2004, pp. 109-130; and: *Spiritual Assessment and Intervention with Older Adults: Current Directions and Applications* (ed: Mark Brennan, and Deborah Heiser) The Haworth Pastoral Press, an imprint of The Haworth Press, Inc., 2004, pp. 109-130. Single or multiple copies of this article are available for a fee from The Haworth Document Delivery Service [1-800-HAWORTH, 9:00 a.m. - 5:00 p.m. (EST). E-mail address: docdelivery@haworthpress.com].

http://www.haworthpress.com/web/JRSA
© 2004 by The Haworth Press, Inc. All rights reserved.
Digital Object Identifier: 10.1300/J496v17n01_06

KEYWORDS. Alzheimer's, spiritual, religious, procedural memory, activities

Lawton (2001) states that there are 11 universal human needs, two of which are meaningful activity and spiritual well-being. These two needs may be fulfilled simultaneously for adults with Alzheimer's disease by specially selected religious activities. Finding the right activities for adults with age-related dementia is also vital to averting disruptive behavior or in simply giving the caregiver a break from providing constant supervision (Gruetzner, 1988; Mace & Rabins, 1991; Vance & Johns, 2002). Given the quadrupling of the prevalence of Alzheimer's disease to 20 million cases in the next 2 decades (Brookmeyer, Gray, & Kawas, 1998), it will become increasingly important to develop effective therapeutic activities.

Due to cognitive impairments associated with Alzheimer's disease and similar dementias, many activities either cannot be done or do not hold the attention span of the adult for any substantial length of time. Kovach and Magliocco (1998) found that residents with late-stage dementia were able to actively participate in activities 10 minutes or less for 54% of the time. When needing help with the activity, caregivers assisted adults 37.5% of the time. In fact, many activities are too difficult or lack the emotional salience to make such participation meaningful to the adult. This results in poor motivation and low levels of engagement in the activity. However, coupled with the high levels of religious participation and involvement in older adults (Ainlay & Smith, 1984; Taylor, 1986; Van Ness & Larson, 2002), and the observed mental and physical health benefits of religious participation (Koenig, George, & Siegler, 1988; Koenig, Kvale, & Ferrel, 1988; Strawbridge, Shema, Cohen, Roberts, & Kaplan, 1998; Taylor, 1986), looking for activities in this arena for adults with Alzheimer's disease promises a likelihood for successful engagement, generalization to this population, and benefit for the individual (Elliot, 1997; Richards & Seicol, 1991). The purpose of this article is to explore the role that religious activity therapy can play for those with Alzheimer's disease. This approach, called Procedural and Emotional Religious Activity Therapy, will be elucidated through using previous studies and examples from different religions. As will be observed, for this approach to be effective, it is important to understand what cognitive abilities are compromised or resistant during the course of Alzheimer's disease.

COGNITIVE COMPONENTS OF RELIGIOUS ACTIVITIES

Five overarching areas are considered in explaining the relevant cognitive domains concomitant with this topic. Executive skills, sensory/perceptual processing, and explicit memory skills are compromised early in the course of the disease. Procedural memory skills and emotional attachment are largely spared during most of the disease process. Thus, activities that focus on existing skills or are modified to account for damaged abilities are apt to be used more effectively in adults with Alzheimer's disease. Also, the stage of the disease at which the person is living reflects their cognitive state in each of these areas.

Executive functioning consists of planning ability, conscious thought, concentration and attention, reallocating cognitive ability, reasoning, and problem-solving. Executive functioning is considered a complex ability that is quickly disrupted by Alzheimer's disease (Cahn-Wiener, Ready, & Malloy, 2003; Grigsby, Kaye, & Robbins, 1995). Thus, spiritual activities that require the use of this ability are likely to be met with failure or frustration. Such highly demanding cognitive activities include intense scriptural study, intense or interactive prayer, and deep meditation. These activities intuitively require focused thought, attention, and concentration. Given the general impairments in executive functioning, these activities will be difficult to perform for participants with Alzheimer's disease during all stages.

Explicit memory skills atrophy quickly in Alzheimer's disease. Explicit memory allows one to consciously recall information. Information stored for shorter periods of time is quickly forgotten because it is not deeply encoded in neural pathways. Information that is stored for longer periods of time is more resistant, probably due to the well-rehearsed nature of the information (Kuzis, Sabe, Tiberti, Merello, Leiguarda, & Starkstein, 1999; Nebes, 1992). For example, childhood memories are a common topic for someone with Alzheimer's disease because of their continued ability to recall information from this period; childhood memories are well-rehearsed and have been encoded for long periods of time. In early and middle stages of Alzheimer's disease, a person can recall an event that happened 20 years ago with vivid detail while being unable to report what he or she had for breakfast earlier that day. For this reason, activities that focus on memories from the past may have a better chance of being utilized than activities that focus on the more recent past.

Perceptual and sensory processing declines are disproportionately observed in adults with Alzheimer's disease. With disease progression, declines in each sensory modality can occur. Visual perceptual difficulties are observed in the middle to later stages of the disease. Such visual perceptional changes include the inability to mentally rotate objects, orient spatially, and process complex visual stimuli (Schneider & Pichora-Fuller, 2000). This may be expressed in such things as getting lost in one's house or manipulating complex objects such as a puzzle. Unless the person already has hearing loss, auditory difficulties are expressed in Alzheimer's disease through impairments in perceptual processing. Even early in the disease, words may sometimes be perceived differently,[1] resulting in miscommunication that leads to agitation (Vance, Burgio, Roth, Stevens, Fairchild, & Yurick, 2003; Gruetzner, 1988). Therefore, clearly spoken language is important to avert this. Olfactory declines are observed early in Alzheimer's disease, such that a normal odor must be increased up to nine times its normal concentration for it to be perceived (Nordin & Murphy, 1996; Vance, 1999). Meanwhile, age-related declines in other modalities such as taste and touch are observed; such declines in Alzheimer's disease do not appear to be particularly problematic. From this, activities that accentuate sensory stimuli have a better chance of being utilized effectively for adults with dementia.

Procedural memory represents those abilities that are done unconsciously, without conscious thought, such as riding a bike, using social graces such as automatically saying "thank you," or twisting a doorknob given the appropriate social or environmental cues. These abilities are highly resistant during the course of the disease and undergo degradation during the final period of the disease (Gabrieli, 1998; Hirono, Mori, Ikejiri, Imamura, Shimomura, Ikeda, Yamashita, Takatsuki, Tokimasa, & Yamadori, 1997; Nebes, 1992). Spiritual activities that rely on this ability are more likely to be done with some amount of success. This includes singing a familiar song or hymn, holding or reciting the Rosary, making the sign of the cross, or holding a sacred object (e.g., scripture book, artifact, symbol). Since procedural memory ability is relatively spared during most of Alzheimer's disease, activities that rely heavily on the use of this cognitive ability will likely be performed successfully.

Finally, emotional processing denotes the ability to form and experience salient connections of a visceral or intuitive nature. Essential to this area are feelings of attachment, fear, happiness, anger, disgust, and surprise. Developmentally, our first task as infants is to attach to our caregiver to ensure survival (Ainsworth, Blehar, Waters, & Wall, 1978). Viewing Alzheimer's disease as a type of reverse ontogeny or backwards development, one of the last surviving abilities is attachment. Because emotional processing is relatively spared during the course of the disease, these activities will be salient and motivating for the participant to engage (Baker, 1996; Borod & Koff, 1989). Thus, the emotional component linked to religious activities ensures that using them will be motivating and comforting to the person. Such general activities include being soothed by a familiar song, feeling secure performing a religious ritual such as holding and reciting a Rosary, and being awed by holding an item associated with one's faith.

The Pattern of Decline in Alzheimer's Disease

As mentioned earlier, each of these cognitive abilities decline at different rates during the disease process. Alzheimer's disease can be roughly categorized into three primary stages–early, middle, and late. The Mini-Mental Status Exam (MMSE), one of the most commonly used measures in gerontology, can be administered to affected adults in order to approximate the stage they are mentally. The MMSE is a brief measure of mental functioning that tests visual-spatial ability, working memory, temporal and spatial orientation, and rudimentary daily skills (Folstein, Folstein, & McHugh, 1975). Scores range from 0 to 30 with higher scores indicating better cognitive functioning. While older adults without dementia score perfectly or nearly perfect on this measure, those in the early stages of Alzheimer's disease may score between 20 and 25. In fact, to exclude people with possible Alzheimer's disease, many studies use a score of 25 or higher to recruit only cognitively intact elders (e.g., Edwards, Wadley, Myers, Roenker, Cissell, & Ball, 2002). During this early stage, the adult may experience deficits in instrumental activities of daily living such as paying bills, driving, and remembering to take medications. Periods of confusion and agitation may also occur. Cognitive declines emerge in multiple areas including detection and identification of odors, short-term memory, explicit or conscious memory, attention, and learning new materials. Spared abilities include procedural (i.e., rote or automatic) memory skills (e.g., using a pencil, catching a ball), emotional processing, classical conditioning, and olfactory detection if the odor is of sufficient concentration (Baker, 1990; Nebes, 1992; Vance, 1999).

A score between 10 and 20 on the MMSE indicates the middle stage of the disease. This stage is characterized by agitation, severe short-term memory loss, some long-term memory loss, and an increased need with personal Activities of Daily Living (ADL) such as bathing and dressing.

Impaired abilities also include disruptions in executive functioning and changes in sensory perception such as depth perception (Nebes, 1992; Nordin & Murphy, 1996). Spared abilities include procedural memory skills and emotional processing. Interestingly, a person in this stage often exhibits many of the social graces in which they were accustomed, thus giving them a sense that they are "normal" or unimpaired.

A score of 10 or below on the MMSE marks the last stage of this disease, characterized by severe impairments in ADL functioning and short- and long-term memory. Impaired abilities include the loss of self-recognition, profound short-term and long-term memory loss, moderate sensory and perceptual impairments, and moderate procedural memory loss. Spared abilities include rudimentary motor abilities such as walking and grasping. Unfortunately, near the end of this disease, even basic survival abilities such as swallowing become difficult (Clibbens, 1996).

Religious Activities and Alzheimer's Disease

From this, a basic picture emerges on the cognitive decline of adults with Alzheimer's disease. Short-term memory is compromised early in the disease process; however, procedural memory and emotional processing decline slowly compared to other abilities. With procedural memory, religious activities that were practiced repeatedly during one's life will be retained longer during the disease process. Personal aspects that are emotionally salient, such as one's faith, also are resistant to decline. Therefore, activities that focus on these two cognitive structures ensure them of being effective in mitigating agitation and improving quality of life for the adult.

Cognitive advantages and disadvantages of using religious activities to abate behavior problems and increase participation in adults with dementia are many. First, and most importantly, many rituals and aspects of religious traditions incorporate procedures that have been practiced repetitively over the lifespan. With such extensive practice, many religious activities become automatic in nature and do not require conscious thought or reasoning abilities. As progressive dementia compromises the function of conscious thought and explicit skills through the deterioration of temporal, parietal, and sections of the frontal lobes, procedural memory skills associated with gross and fine motor movement and repetition remain resilient during most of the disease course (Nebes, 1992). Procedural memory skills are available to the adult with Alzheimer's disease to participate in well-practiced rituals. For instance, a Rosary is an excellent activity for a devout Catholic with Alzheimer's disease because he or she can go through the recitation, executing the motor skills of moving the beads, and if language skills are not severely compromised, saying the prayers. Second, attachment and reverence to one's religious traditions and beliefs can remain strong during cognitive decline.

Many of the subcortical structures associated with emotional salience (i.e., conditioned emotional response) and attachment are less influenced by the pathogenesis of Alzheimer's disease (Goldsmith, 2001; Nebes, 1992). Thus, the emotional attachment to religious cueing and corresponding activity can be an implicit source of comfort and joy for the participant with Alzheimer's disease. For example, spinning a dreidel may produce feelings of fun and excitement for an elderly Jewish man who did this in childhood during Hanukkah. Though he may not consciously recall the event, the activity itself can cue the emotional response associated with the task. Finally, since many religious activities are emotionally salient and intrinsically rewarding to adults with a religious background, this provides the motivation that helps capture and hold their participation.

COMPARISON OF RELIGIOUS ACTIVITIES TO OTHER ACTIVITY PARADIGMS

Several approaches in activity therapy are employed that emphasize creating a good fit between the person and the activity. This person-activity fit must balance one's existing abilities with the demands of the activity. The person-activity fit must also satisfy some need such as being useful or enjoyable. While some of the activity paradigms are simply practical in nature, others have theoretical underpinnings that may make them especially efficacious (see Table 1). Traditional activity employs a variety of materials and is eclectic in nature. Such activities include playing bingo, cooking, and gardening. This approach does not possess a theoretical foundation which limits its application. Regardless, advantages of this approach are that it is easy to use and materials are conveniently procured. Regrettably, many of these activities are not very engaging and require continued prompting for people to use them. In addition, many of these activities, such as cooking, may be inappropriate for adults with severe cognitive impairments.

TABLE 1. Advantages and Disadvantages of Activity Paradigms

Activity Paradigm	Advantages	Disadvantages
Traditional/Eclectic Approach	*Easy to use *Materials readily available *Does not require a facilitator	*No explicit theoretical drive *Very stimulating/engaging *Limited to early/middle dementia stages
Sensory Stimulation	*Easy to use *Materials readily available *Theoretical and empirical support *Usable all dementia stages *Does not require a facilitator	*Many sensory declines are mechanistic problems, not perceptual problems *Not very stimulating/engaging
Reality Orientation	*Easy to use *Materials readily available *Theoretical and empirical support	*Activities limited to orientation *Few activities available *Limited to early/middle dementia stages
Reminiscence Therapy	*Materials readily available *Theoretical and empirical support *Focuses on long-term memory, not short-term memory *Emotionally salient	* Requires a facilitator or leader * Requires participants to be verbal * Limited to early/middle dementia stages
Pet Therapy	* Useful with severe cognitive impairments * Empirical support * Usable in all dementia stages	*Requires a facilitator or leader *Pet with trainer is advised *Participants and animals can become dangerously reactive to each other
Music Therapy	* Materials readily available * Easy to use * Theoretical and empirical support * Usually quite engaging * Emotionally salient * Usable in all cognitive stages	*Not effective with participants with hearing impairments *Often requires a facilitator or leader
Montessori Didactic	*Theoretical and empirical support *Can be used in all dementia stages	*Training is required to administer, and materials can be difficult to acquire and expensive *Not necessarily engaging *May require one-on-one attention
Procedural and Emotional-Religious Activity Therapy	*Theoretical and empirical support *Easy to use *Materials readily available *Emotionally salient *Usually quite engaging *Usable in all dementia stages	*Must be individualized *Not useful for those without a religious or spiritual history

Note: Principles and techniques of these activity paradigms overlap with each other.

Sensory Stimulation

Sensory stimulation activities underscore reinitiating the use of certain sensory modalities by exaggerating a selected sensory aspect of a task. For example, bright colorful cardboard shapes may be available for a person with advanced Alzheimer's disease to touch and match with other shapes or colors. The goal of this activity is to facilitate interaction through basic and vivid sensory components, in this case shape and color. This technique is quite simple to use and materials are easily made or obtained. The theoretical underpinning posits that continued stimulation of the senses through activities that specifically target each of the sensory modalities will facilitate neural activity, resulting in maintenance of cognitive functioning (Burnside, 1986). Unfortunately, many sensory declines are due to atrophy of sensory organs, and therefore stimulation of such modalities may not have neural benefits. Also, some of the goals of these activities can be unclear, which may facilitate boredom or frustration.

Reality Orientation

Reality orientation attempts to involve participants with cues in order to promote awareness of self, place, time, and circumstance. Combined with a traditional approach, activities are very basic, such as helping participants recognize the season by engaging them in arts or crafts appropriate for the time such as carving pumpkins near Halloween (Burnside, 1986). Though materials are easy to find and use, many activities can be limiting to adults with severe cognitive impairment and memory impairments.

Reminiscence Therapy

Reminiscence therapy is often a group-oriented approach that requires participants to share thoughts and feelings related to certain topics. The activity can also be done through individualized journal writing (Kelly & Mosher-Ashley, 2002); however, typically the activity is conducted in a group setting by a leader who presents items for discussion. As an item passes from participant to participant, they are asked to interact with the item, recall an associated event, and share their memory with the group (Burnside, 1986). For example, a rose could be presented whereby participants may talk about how they received a rose or gave a rose to someone and share the circumstances surrounding the event.

Theoretically, this approach can be emotionally motivating and focuses on long-term memory that is appropriate for those in early stages of Alzheimer's disease. Unfortunately, this approach requires a skilled group leader as well as requires participants to be verbal enough to share experiences with the group, which can be problematic for those who are reticent. Therefore, this approach is not effective for adults with moderate to severe dementia.

Pet Therapy

Pet therapy employs the use of animals to promote activity, interest, and stimulation. Pet therapy primarily consists of monitoring adults' interaction with a domesticated animal such as a cat or dog (Burnside, 1986; Kanamori et al., 2001). Ordinarily, this is quite motivating given that many people have had exposure to a pet during the course of their life. The advantage of this approach is that it is emotionally salient and motivating, and has been shown to be effective in working with people who have even severe cognitive impairments. The disadvantage is that this activity requires a facilitator, not to mention that animals can become reactive should a participant become agitated or restless.

Music Therapy

As the name suggests, music therapy uses music as a means to involve participants and promote activity. This activity consists of having participants sing along, use rudimentary instruments such as drumsticks, tambourines, and bells, or simply listen to music in the background (Burnside, 1986; Matthews, Clair, & Kosloski, 2001). Obvious advantages of this approach include that it is easy to incorporate in multiple settings, is enjoyable, has vast appeal, and has theoretical and empirical support. Additionally, this approach can be used during all stages of dementia, making it very beneficial. Regrettably, hearing impairments are common in the elderly population (Bergman & Rosenhall, 2001), limiting the efficacy of this approach.

Montessori Techniques

Montessori is a didactic that has recently been adapted for Alzheimer's disease because it mirrors Piagetian concepts of mental development. In recent years, it has been employed with participants with Alzheimer's disease, focusing on the concept of reverse ontogeny. Activities consist of ADLs that employ procedural memory skills; however, activities also include cognitive tasks that highlight specific cognitive tasks such as gradation. For instance, an adult may be given several blue tiles of various shades and be asked to line them up from lighter to darker. If the conceptual ability of gradation is still viable in the person, the hope and assumption of this approach is that the adult will sort these tiles automatically. The advantages of this approach are that it has strong theoretical and empirical support, can be used at all stages, and uses a variety of materials (Vance & Johns, 2002; Vance & Porter, 2000). Disadvantages are that it requires training to administer the materials, some materials are difficult to make or expensive to buy, and may require one-on-one attention.

Empirical Support for Procedural and Emotional Religious Therapy

Clearly, aspects of Procedural and Emotional Religious Activity Therapy are already present in the literature; however, its cognitive advantages have not been vocalized. Regardless, previous studies on activity therapy have demonstrated the efficacy of religious activities in providing improved quality of life and mitigating agitation and restlessness in this population. Stolley and colleagues (Stolley, Koenig, & Buckwalter, 1999) emphasized the manner with which using religious activities with adults with Alzheimer's disease incorporates aspects of the Progressively Lowered Stress Threshold model. This model states that dysfunctional behavior in demented elders can be the result of increased negative activity that is associated with environmental stimuli that exceeds their level of tolerance. Thus, the provision for a low-stimulus environment should reduce anxiety and, thereby, reduce the exhibition of disruptive behavior. Thus, spiritual activities may reduce anxiety by providing a safe and pleasant activity, resulting in prosocial behavior.

Several studies support the effectiveness of this approach. Abramowitz (1993) incorporated morning prayers as part of normal activity in four adults day cares in Israel with mentally impaired Jewish elders. Prayer sessions last from 10 to 15 minutes with only the most familiar prayers being used. The hazan, or cantor, reads the prayer aloud. Anecdotal reports confirm that while participants may not retain a conscious recollection of the prayer, they maintain an emotional connection to this spiritual activity. Similarly, Jennings and Vance (2002) provided music sessions to participants with Alzheimer's disease in an adult day care setting. Musical selections included only popular, familiar music known by the participants. Musical selections focused heavily on songs with strong religious or patriotic content. It was observed that agitation levels decreased for participants.

Khouzam and colleagues (Khouzam, Smith, & Bissett, 1994) presented a case study of two veterans in a nursing home. Upon doing a personal religious assessment, researchers found key Bible verses that had particular emotional appeal to each person. Staff then recited these verses to each participant over a 6-week period during the first signs of agitation. The number of agitated episodes decreased dramatically for both. Thus, given the theoretical framework of cognitive functioning and past research on the calming effects of religious activities in adults with Alzheimer's disease, it is clear that research in this area should be extended to all religious paradigms.

ACTIVITIES OF RELIGIOUS PARADIGMS

With the diversity of religious and spiritual expressions, it is unrealistic to provide examples of how to apply this technique to every persuasion. In an attempt to be inclusive, general examples of appropriate and inappropriate activities from the major world religions are suggested. Further, Catholic and Protestant distinctions in Christianity are provided to reflect the readership. Otherwise, generalizations of all the major religions are made.

Hinduism

Hinduism is a polytheistic system of thought that focuses on the cycles of life and death and transcendence into the actual realms of reality through right action and meditation. Albeit, key concepts such as karma, reincarnation, and Dharma are similar to such concepts found in Buddhism, Hinduism has a much stronger focus on reverence for a pantheon of deities such as Brahman and Vishnu (Nielsen, Hein, Reynolds, Miller, Karff, Cochran, & McLeon, 1983). For a Hindu with Alzheimer's disease, certain religious activities may be particularly advantageous given that they are easy to do and require procedural memory abilities such as yoga, puja, and chanting.

The movement component of yoga, if the person is well practiced, can be applied given that this is well rehearsed and does not require explicit memory; however, given demands on attention and concentration, prompts during this particular activity may be necessary. Puja is the shrine in a private home. The image in the shrine is offered food, water, and incense. Activities can focus on preparing offerings around the Puja. Finally, chanting the name of a deity, or Om for short, can be a simple activity for someone given it is well practiced and possesses deep spiritual significance.

Buddhism

Buddhism is a polytheistic system of belief that emphasizes right actions and thoughts in order to transcend the corporeal (illusory) and enter the spiritual (real) world. This is a system that is thought to have developed from Janism and Hinduism. This religion centers on the Buddha, also known as Siddhartha. Siddhartha entered a state of enlightenment when he was 34 years old, and lived the remainder of his life on earth teaching others. Those who reach such enlightenment are also known as Buddhas or Bodhisattvas (Bukkyó Dendó Kyókai, 1993; Nielsen et al., 1983).

For a Buddhist with Alzheimer's disease, several activities may be done that are appropriate because they also use procedural and emotional memory and require little explicit memory or skill to do. Such activities include prayer wheels, prayer flags, and maintaining shrines. Prayer wheels are cylinders mounted on an axle. Prayers are written on the cylinder and as they are spun, the prayer is transmitted. Therefore, spinning a prayer wheel is a simple act that still offers meaning. In Tibetan Buddhism, prayer flags can be made and tied to a tree or pole. Activity can focus on creating such a prayer flag and securing it. Shrines to one of the many Buddhas are a fundamental aspect of reverence; such shrines are common in the homes of believers. Therefore, building a shrine to Buddha out of reverence and servicing the shrine with appropriate offerings of incense and food (depending upon the tradition) would be an appropriate activity for the Alzheimer's patient.

Judaism

Judaism is a monotheistic system of thinking whereby it is believed that God provided his people with a set way of living and conducting their lives (Nielsen et al., 1983). For a Jew with Alzheimer's disease, the following may be appropriate religious activities: Spinning a dreidel, singing sacred songs or hymns, holding a sacred object or icons (e.g., Star of David, yarmulke, Torah), or reciting familiar scripture (e.g., Ten Commandments). During holiday seasons such as Hanukkah, lighting of the menorah can also be done with supervision.

Christian Traditions

Catholicism is a monotheistic system of thinking that espouses the forgiveness of sin through Jesus Christ and acknowledges the authority of the Holy Roman Catholic Church (Nielsen et al., 1983). For a Catholic with Alzheimer's disease, several activities may be used appropriately given their well-practiced or deeply meaningful significance. As mentioned earlier, recitation of the Rosary can be done effectively given its repetitive and calming nature. For someone in the early stages of Alzheimer's disease, recitation of response readings is also appropriate. Ritualistic prayers can be incorporated given the highly familiar nature of the task. Thus, those in the early stages of the disease can conduct a perpetual novena, a ritual involving lighting a candle and focusing a prayer on a particular request. Of course, holding a religious icon or singing or humming sacred songs can provide emotional comfort to someone throughout the course of the disease.

Protestantism is a monotheistic system of thinking that espouses the forgiveness of sin through Jesus Christ (Balmer, 1993; Nielsen et al., 1983). More emphasis on individual interpretation of the Bible is provided than in Catholicism. Likewise, similar activities can be done. Singing sacred songs or hymns, holding religious symbols or icons such as the Bible, or reciting favorite or popular scriptures (for example, Psalms 23; 1 Corinthians 13; The Beatitudes; The Lord's Prayer; The Ten Commandments) are all appropriate activities. As can be done with many other religions, using arts and crafts to focus on a particular belief is appropriate. For example, religious coloring books and looking through religious artwork can be implemented with ease.

Islam

Islam is a monotheistic system of belief whereby God will weigh the actions, whether it be good or evil, of people and pronounce judgment accordingly. Strict rules of behavior for individuals and society are the norm (Nielsen et al., 1983). For a Muslim with Alzheimer's disease, the following activities may be appropriate given their familiarity, emotional salience, and repetition: facing towards Mecca to pray (a.k.a., Salah), singing of sacred songs or hymns, holding of religious symbols or icon such as the Koran.

General Guidelines Regardless of Religious Affiliation

Across all of these religions, those activities that require explicit memory skills, attention, and concentration should be avoided for someone with Alzheimer's disease. Inappropriate activities include intense scriptural study and focused meditation since these require good working memory and concentration. Other activities like pilgrimages, such as Hajj (i.e., pilgrimage to Mecca), are obviously rigorous endeavors for someone who is well, and would be extremely problematic for someone with Alzheimer's disease. Meanwhile, activities that are repetitive, require motor movements, and have simple meaning are more likely to be engaging for someone with Alzheimer's disease. The above provides only a gross examination of this approach for each of these religious traditions. Obviously, a much more detailed examination for each paradigm should be considered in further discussion and studies.

CONSIDERATIONS WHEN USING RELIGIOUS ACTIVITIES

Obvious disadvantages and caveats to this approach must be stated. First, many other religious activities utilize highly focused cognitive skills such as Bible studies, deep meditation as in Buddhism, and elaborate storytelling as is part of the oral tradition for many religions. Therefore, exposure to such intellectual activities may confuse or frustrate participants with Alzheimer's disease. Second, partitioning religious activities into procedural and explicit cognitive tasks requires intimate knowledge of the religious activity and of cognitive systems. Such a task analysis would require breaking down the activity into its constituent parts and classifying the cognitive demands for each part. Nursing home and adult day care activity therapists would need training about cognitive systems and religious paradigms in order to find appropriate activities for their participants.

Third, not all older adults have participated heavily in a religious tradition or belief system; such adults will likely not benefit from this approach. In some cases, a participant may have left a particular religious paradigm due to ideological objections or traumatic experiences associated with it. Exposing religious cues and activities to such a participant with Alzheimer's disease may facilitate a catastrophic behavior. Thus, knowledge of the participant's religious history is necessary not only to implement this approach, but also to prevent harm. To obtain such knowledge, a Prior Religious Involvement Inventory (see Appendix A) will need to be administered to family members.

Fourth, for the participant who has participated in a religious paradigm, depending on the zeal of the person, he or she may become too enthusiastic in reaction to the religious content of the activity. For example, listening to the tenor of a sermon may fill an adult with a sense of holy indignation. Such a heightened emotional state may act as an antecedent to a host of behavioral problems. Finally, this approach cannot readily be applied to all cognitively impaired adults. Hemispheric lesions as caused in cerebrovascular accidents have been shown to exhibit differential deficits in emotional processing. In fact, electroencephalogram data suggests that positive and negative emotion perception and processing are lateralized in respect to left and right frontal cortical areas, respectively (Borod & Koff, 1989; Heilman, Watson, & Bowers, 1983). Therefore, this approach would only be effective depending upon the size and placement of the cerebrovascular incident. Similarly, other dementias such as Huntington's disease compromise subcortical structures that impair the participant's ability to comprehend both emotional prosody and verbal description of emotion (Speedic, Brake, Folstein, & Bowers, 1990). Thus, the neuropsychiatric features of Huntington's disease prevent this approach from being effective in the same manner.

CONCLUSION AND IMPLICATIONS

In conclusion, given the proper precautions, the benefits from this approach in producing a set of activities for adults with Alzheimer's disease seem great. This perspective on activities for adults with Alzheimer's disease should advance by first conducting case studies and then progressing to experimental designs in adult day programs, nursing homes, and familial caregivers. The potential for reduced behavioral disturbances for the participant and increased quality of life for both caregiver and the care recipient show merit and warrant further investigation.

Although using religious activities in adults with Alzheimer's disease is not new, understanding the cognitive application of these activities is. Research in this area can be explored in several venues. First, to determine whether this approach would be appropriate for a participant, a religious history assessment as suggested earlier needs to be developed and tested (see Appendix A). Second, a curriculum to train activity therapists how to identify which religious and spiritual activities would be appropriate for the mental condition and personal history of the participant needs to be developed. Third, behavioral programs and behavioral prescriptions as seen in the literature (Cotter, Stevens, Vance, & Burgio, 2000) can also capitalize upon this approach (see Appendix B). For example, religious activities can be used to abate or mitigate agitation and facilitate active involvement and motility.

Fourth, religious activities can be used as a part of environmental design. For example, Cohen-Mansfield and Werner (1998) created two nature scenes consisting of a mural, nature sounds such as birds chirping, and an aroma machine that emitted nature scents. These scenes were placed in sections of a hallway to reduce wandering in adults with Alzheimer's disease. The same approach could be adapted with religious overtones. For instance, a religious mural along with sacred items such as an altar, and accompanying symbols, could be used to create a soothing, spiritual nook. Concomitant religious music and incense, if appropriate, could also be included provided participants are able to hear and incense is of sufficient concentration. Carnes (2001) reported using a similar technique in which votive candles, spiritual music, and a religious canvas were used to create a place of peace for older adults with Alzheimer's disease. Fifth, a major challenge is how to bridge this approach to secular environments in which adults of various religious background are present. Finally, research will need to explore if this technique is effective with other forms of dementia such as vascular dementia and Parkinson's disease. In conclusion, this approach holds much potential in improving the quality of life for adults affected by Alzheimer's disease.

NOTE

1. Receptive Aphasia-A neurological phenomenon whereby words are perceived as different words due to damage of the language areas of the brain (e.g., Wernicke's area).

REFERENCES

Abramowitz, L. (1993). Prayer as therapy among the frail Jewish elderly. *Journal of Gerontological Social Work, 19* (3/4), 69-75.

Ainlay, S. C., & Smith, D. R. (1984). Aging and religious participation. *Journal of Gerontology, 39* (3), 357-363.

Ainsworth, M. D. S., Blehar, M. C., Waters, E., & Wall, S. (1978). *Patterns of attachment.* Hillsdale, NJ: Lawrence Erlbaum Associates.

Baker, J. G. (1996). Memory and emotional processing in cortical and subcortical dementia. *The Journal of General Psychology, 123* (3), 185-191.

Balmer, R. (1993). *Mine eyes have seen the glory: A journey into the evangelical subculture of America.* New York: Oxford University Press.

Bergman, B., & Rosenhall, U. (2001). Vision and hearing in old age. *Scandinavian Audiology, 30* (4), 255-263.

Borod, J. C., & Koff, E. (1989). The neuropsychology of emotion: Evidence from normal, neurological, and psychiatric populations. In E. Perecman (Ed.), *Integrating theory and practice in clinical neuropsychology.* Hillsdale, NJ: Lawrence Erlbaum Associates, Publishers.

Brookmeyer, R., Gray, S., & Kawas, C. (1998). Projections of Alzheimer's disease in the United States and the public health impact of delaying disease onset. *American Journal of Public Health, 88,* 1337-1342.

Bukkyō Dendō Kyōkai (1993). *The teaching of Buddha.* Tokyo, Japan: Kosaido.

Burnside, I. (1986). *Working with the elderly: Group process & techniques* (2nd ed.). Boston, MA: Jones and Bartlett Publishers, Inc.

Cahn-Weiner, D. A., Ready, R. E., & Malloy, P. F. (2003). Neuropsychological predictors of everyday memory and everyday functioning in patients with mild Alzheimer's disease. *Journal of Geriatric Psychiatry & Neurology, 16* (2), 84-89.

Carnes, V. B. (2001). Walking the labyrinth of peace. *Nursing Homes Long Term Care Management, 50* (10), 41-42.

Clibbens, R. (1996). Eating, ethics, and Alzheimer's. *Nursing Times, 92* (50), 29-30.

Cohen-Mansfield, J., & Werner, P. (1998). The effects of an enhanced environment on nursing home residents who pace. *The Gerontologist, 38,* 199-208.

Cotter, E. M., Stevens, A., Vance, D. E., & Burgio, L. D. (2000). Caregiver skills training in problem solving. *Alzheimer's Care Quarterly, 1* (4), 50-61.

Edwards, J. D., Wadley, V. G., Myers, R. S., Roenker, D. L., Cissell, G. M., & Ball, K. K. (2002). Transfer of a speed of processing intervention to near and far cognitive functions. *Gerontology, 48,* 329-340.

Elliot, H. (1997). Religion, spirituality, and dementia: Pasturing to sufferers of Alzheimer's disease and other associated forms of dementia. *Disability & Rehabilitation, 19* (10), 435-441.

Folstein, M. F., Folstein, S. E., & McHugh, P. R. (1975). "MINI-MENTAL STATE": A practical method for grading the cognitive state of participants for the clinician. *Journal of Psychiatric Rehabilitation, 12,* 189-198.

Gabrieli, J. D. (1998). Cognitive neuroscience of human memory. *Annual Review of Psychology, 49,* 87-115.

Goldsmith, M. (2001). When words are no longer necessary: The gift of ritual. *Journal of Religious Gerontology, 12* (3-4), 139-150.

Grigsby, J., Kaye, K., & Robbins, L. J. (1995). Behavioral disturbance and impairment of executive functions among the elderly. *Archives of Gerontology and Geriatrics, 21* (2), 167-177.

Gruetzner, H. (1988). *Alzheimer's: A caregiver's guide and source book.* New York, NY: John Wiley & Sons.

Heilman, K. M., Watson, R. T., & Bowers, D. (1983). Affective disorders associated with hemispheric disease. In K. M. Heilman and P. Satz (Eds.), *Neuropsychology of human emotion*. New York: Guilford Press.

Hirono, N., Mori, E., Ikejiri, Y., Imamura, T., Shimomura, T., Ikeda, M., Yamashita, H., Takatsuki, Y., Tokimasa, A., & Yamadori, A. (1997). Procedural memory in patients with mild Alzheimer's disease. *Dementia & Geriatric Cognitive Disorders, 8* (4), 210-216.

Jennings, B., & Vance, D. (2002). The short-term effects of music therapy on different types of agitation in adults with Alzheimer's. *Activities, Adaptation, & Aging, 26* (4), 27-33.

Kanamori, M., Suzuki, M., Yamamoto, K., Kanda, M., Matsui, Y., Kojima, E., Fukawa, H., Sugita, T., & Oshiro, H. (2001). A day care program and evaluation of animal-assisted therapy (AAT) for the elderly with senile dementia. *American Journal of Alzheimer's Disease, 16* (4), 234-239.

Kelly, L. M., & Mosher-Ashley, P. M. (2002). Combining reminiscence with journal writing to promote greater life satisfaction in an assisted-living community. *Activities, Adaptation, & Aging, 26* (4), 35-46.

Khouzam, H. R., Smith, C. E., & Bissett, B. (1994). Bible therapy: A treatment of agitation in elderly patients with Alzheimer's disease. *Clinical Gerontologist, 15* (2), 71-74.

Koenig, H. G., George, L. K., & Siegler, I. C. (1988). The use of religion and other emotion-regulating coping strategies among older adults. *The Gerontologist, 28* (3), 303-310.

Koenig, H. G., Kvale, J. N., & Ferrel, C. (1988). Religion and well-being in later life. *The Gerontologist, 28* (1), 18-28.

Kovach, C. R., & Magliocco, J. S. (1998). Late-stage dementia and participation in therapeutic activities. *Applied Nursing Research, 11* (4), 167-173.

Kuzis, G., Sabe, L., Tiberti, C., Merello, M., Leiguarda, R., & Starkstein, S. E. (1999). Explicit and implicit learning in patients with Alzheimer disease and Parkinson disease with dementia. *Neuropsychiatry, Neuropsychology, & Behavioral Neurology, 12* (4), 265-269.

Lawton, M. P. (2001). Physical environment of the person with Alzheimer's disease. *Aging and Mental Health, 5* (Suppl. 1), S56-S64.

Mace, N. L., & Rabins, P. V. (1991). *The 36-hour day* (revised ed.). Baltimore, MD: The Johns Hopkins University Press.

Matthews, R. M., Clair, A. A., & Kosloski, K. (2001). Keeping the beat: Use of rhythmic music during exercise activities for the elderly with dementia. *American Journal of Alzheimer's Disease and Other Dementia, 16* (6), 377-380.

Nebes, R. D. (1992). Cognitive dysfunction in Alzheimer's disease. In F. I. M. Craik, & T. A. Salthouse (Eds.), *The handbook of aging and cognition* (pp. 373-446). Hillsdale, NJ: Lawrence Erlbaum Associates, Publishers.

Nielsen, N. C., Hein, N., Reynolds, F. E., Miller, A. L., Karff, S. E., Cochran, A. C., & McLeon, P. (1983). *Religions of the world*. New York: St. Martin's Press.

Nordin, S., & Murphy, C. (1996). Impaired sensory and cognitive olfactory function in questionable Alzheimer's disease. *Neuropsychology, 10* (1), 113-119.

Richards, M., & Seicol, S. (1991). Challenge of maintaining spiritual connectedness for persons institutionalized with dementia. *Journal of Religious Gerontology, 7* (3), 27-40.

Schneider, B. A., & Pichora-Fuller, M. K. (2000). Implication of perceptual deterioration for cognitive aging research (pp. 155-219). In F. I. M. Craik & T. A. Salthouse (Eds.), *The handbook of aging and cognition* (2nd ed.). Mahwah, NJ: Lawrence Erlbaum Associates.

Speedic, L. J., Brake, N., Folstein, S. E., & Bowers, D. (1990). Comprehension of prosody in Huntington's disease. *Journal of Neurology, Neurosurgery, and Psychiatry, 53,* 607-610.

Stolley, J. M., Koenig, H., & Buckwalter, K. C. (1999). Pastoral care for the person with dementia. *Journal of Health Care Chaplaincy, 8* (1/2), 7-23.

Strawbridge, W. J., Shema, S. J., Cohen, R. D., Roberts, R. E., & Kaplan, G. A. (1998). Religiosity buffers effects of some stressors on depression but exacerbates others. *Journal of Gerontology, 53B* (3), S118-S126.

Taylor, R. J. (1986). Religious participation among elderly blacks. *The Gerontologist, 26,* 630-636.

Van Ness, P. H., & Larson, D. B. (2002). Religion, senescence, and mental health: The end of life is not the end of hope. *American Journal of Geriatric Psychiatry, 10* (4), 386-397.

Vance, D. (1999). Considering olfactory stimulation for adults with age-related dementia. *Perceptual & Motor Skills, 88,* 398-400.

Vance, D. E., Burgio, L. D., Roth, D. L., Stevens, A. B., Fairchild, J. K., & Yurick, A. (2003). Predictors of agitation in nursing home residents. *Journal of Gerontology, 58B,* P129-P137.

Vance, D. E., & Johns, R. N. (2002). Montessori improved cognitive domains in adults with Alzheimer's disease. *Physical & Occupational Therapy in Geriatrics, 20* (3/4), 19-36.

Vance, D. E., & Porter, R. J., Jr. (2000). Cognitive benefits from using Montessori in Alzheimer's day cares. *Activities, Adaptation & Aging, 24* (3), 1-22.

APPENDIX A

Prior Religious Involvement Inventory

1. What is the participant's current religious persuasion? (Be specific.)

2. How long has the participant been involved in their faith?

3. Is the participant affiliated with a body of believers such as a church or temple?

4. If so, how active were they?

5. Was the participant born into this faith or did they convert later in life? If later, when did the participant convert and why?

6. If the participant did convert, what was the participant's previous religious persuasion?

7. How devoted to their faith was the participant?

8. Does the participant have any unresolved issues of his/her faith?

9. What were some of the religious activities that the participant particularly enjoyed?

10. What were some of the religious activities that the participant particularly disliked?

11. What were some of the religious activities that the participant did quite often?

12. What were some of the religious activities that the participant did infrequently?

13. Does the participant still have any religious books, possessions, or icons that have particular meaning to him/her?

APPENDIX B

Behavioral Prescription Using Religious Activities

Background: Mr. G. (a 73-year-old African American male) is in the middle stages of Alzheimer's disease and has an MMSE score of 15. Cared for by his daughter in her house, the participant has good hearing but has trouble seeing objects in the distance. The participant is ambulatory. The participant was a life-long member of the Baptist church. The caregiver reports that her father wanders around the house while she is doing housework, shadows her, becomes fidgety and agitated, and does not engage in activities.

BEHAVIORAL PRESCRIPTION
Target Behavior: Low Activity Level/Restlessness

Low Level Activity Defined-When Mr. G. sits on the couch and stares into space.

Restlessness Defined-When Mr. G. tries to leave the house, gets angry or nervous, looks for his car keys, or shadows caregiver.

Prescription to Change the Antecedents:

1. Have at least three activities planned for Mr. G. everyday. Activities can include religious coloring books, religious picture books, making crosses with sticks, listening to a taped sermon from his church, or listening to religious music.
2. Have all the materials needed for the activity ready to be used instantly.
3. Have some activities that involve exercise such as moving around clapping or swaying with the upbeat or soothing gospel music.
4. Track the use of these activities on a chart on the refrigerator to determine which ones work the best.

Prescription to Cope with Behavior:

1. When restlessness occurs, have three salient and motivating activities that are ready to be used. Use an upbeat gospel tape and a soothing gospel tape for him to listen to. Place it in the stereo cabinet and mark it "Happy Gospel" and "Relaxing Gospel" to help you identify these tapes quickly. When Mr. G. becomes restless, play one of the tapes for five minutes and begin singing with him. If that tape does not work, try other tapes and sing with him.
2. Record a sermon from his church and keep it with the other tapes. When Mr. G. becomes agitated or restless, play the sermon and give him his grandmother's Bible to hold and remind him to listen to the sermon.

Prescription to Change Consequences:

1. Praise Mr. G. when he participates in an activity.
2. Remember that it is not important how much Mr. G. gets done or how well he does it. The goal is to help him remain active and as involved as he possibly can.
3. When Mr. G. is agitated, restless, or withdraws, try one of the activities you have planned.

Spirituality and Palliative Care:
The CARE Cabinet Intervention

Deborah Heiser, PhD
Mark Brennan, PhD
John Redic II, MDiv

SUMMARY. The "Creating Alternative Relaxing Environment (CARE) Cabinet" intervention was designed to complement existing palliative care services and addresses the spiritual and socialization needs of patients and family members in conjunction with pastoral care in an institutional setting. The portable CARE Cabinet contains a variety of materials to foster spiritual wellness (e.g., reading materials, audio [i.e., music and nature sounds], aromatherapy), and social interaction (e.g.,

---

Deborah Heiser is Research Associate, Isabella Geriatric Center, 515 Audubon Avenue, New York, NY 10040 (E-mail: dheiser@isabella.org). Mark Brennan is Senior Research Associate, Arlene R. Gordon Research Institute of Lighthouse International, 111 East 59th Street, New York, NY 10022-1202 (E-mail: mbrennan@lighthouse.org). John Redic II is Director of Pastoral Services, Isabella Geriatric Center, 515 Audubon Avenue, New York, NY 10040 (E-mail: jredic@isabella.org).

The authors would like to thank Joel Weinberger and Thalia MacMillan for their comments on an earlier version of this article.

Portions of this paper were presented at the symposium, "Meeting the Needs of Older Adults through Spirituality Assessment and Intervention" (M. Brennan and D. Heiser, Organizers) at the 56th Annual Scientific Meeting of the Gerontological Society of America, November, 2003, San Diego, CA.

[Haworth co-indexing entry note]: "Spirituality and Palliative Care: The CARE Cabinet Intervention." Heiser, Deborah, Mark Brennan, and John Redic II. Co-published simultaneously in *Journal of Religion, Spirituality & Aging* (The Haworth Pastoral Press, an imprint of The Haworth Press, Inc.) Vol. 17, No. 1/2, 2004, pp. 131-149; and: *Spiritual Assessment and Intervention with Older Adults: Current Directions and Applications* (ed: Mark Brennan, and Deborah Heiser) The Haworth Pastoral Press, an imprint of The Haworth Press, Inc., 2004, pp. 131-149. Single or multiple copies of this article are available for a fee from The Haworth Document Delivery Service [1-800-HAWORTH, 9:00 a.m. - 5:00 p.m. (EST). E-mail address: docdelivery@haworthpress.com].

snacks for patient and visitors, visitor meal coupons, facility contact lists). Results of this intervention have been overwhelmingly positive. In one case, the resident used the audio and aromatherapy, while his wife read the Bible, allowing each individual to pursue spiritual activities that provided the most comfort. The snacks and meal coupons encouraged other family members to visit the resident regularly, mitigating his social isolation. In other cases, conversations concerning spiritual issues between the care recipient and pastoral care providers and volunteers have been facilitated by the CARE Cabinet contents. Implications of this intervention for end-of-life care are discussed and its continued application in this and other settings is recommended. *[Article copies available for a fee from The Haworth Document Delivery Service: 1-800-HAWORTH. E-mail address: <docdelivery@haworthpress.com> Website: <http://www. HaworthPress. com> © 2004 by The Haworth Press, Inc. All rights reserved.]*

KEYWORDS. Spiritual wellness, palliative care, end-of-life, bereavement, social interaction

Nearly one-in-five deaths occur in nursing home settings at present, and this proportion is expected to increase with the aging of the population (Ersek & Wilson, 2003). Because death is regularly thought of as strictly a physical process, the emotional and spiritual aspects of dying are often overlooked. The failure to address these psychosocial needs in nursing home settings has been identified as one of the factors that may hamper the provision of high quality end-of-life care to nursing home residents (Ersek & Wilson, 2003).

The palliative care paradigm, whose origins can be traced to the hospice movement of the last few decades, has been adopted in nursing home settings to better address the physical and psychosocial needs of patients needing end-of-life care and their families (Rumbold, 2003). Palliative care is aimed at relieving suffering and optimizing the life quality of terminally ill patients by controlling symptoms, maximizing psychosocial well-being, and addressing spiritual concerns (Perron & Schonwetter, 2001; Twycross, 2002). Patients should be considered as whole persons when being served by healing professionals, especially in palliative care settings (Davies, Brenner, Orloff, Sumner, & Worden, 2002; Sulmasy, 2002). Patients at the end of life *do* want their spiritual needs addressed, especially those who were religious to begin with (Sulmasy, 2002). As a result, addressing spiritual concerns is considered to be a fundamental element in the provision of palliative care from this holistic perspective (Perron & Schonwetter; Rumbold, 2001).

Spiritual Concerns Among Palliative Care Patients and Families

In the process of trying to cope with impending death, the terminally ill patient is faced with the additional challenge of trying to maintain psychosocial and spiritual well-being in order to maximize quality of life during the time before death. Rumbold (2003) notes that facing the prospects of imminent death along with the physical and psychosocial changes concomitant with terminal illness leads the patient and significant others to reflect on fundamental spiritual issues of life, such as life's purpose and meaning, as well as expectations around the end of life. Rumbold also remarks that spiritual needs may emerge in multitudinous ways, for example, while trying to cope with physical changes or through the practice of religious and spiritual beliefs and rituals.

According to Rumbold (2003), spirituality involves not only our sense of purpose and meaning in life, and the ability to transcend one's circumstances, but also encompasses the "web of relationships" that constitute our social support network, namely, family and significant others, community groups and organizations. Sometimes during the period preceding death, close family and well-meaning friends withdraw adding to the trauma and sense of loss. The disruption of these ties following the onset of terminal illness results in a sense of vulnerability and disconnection.

The National Cancer Institute (2002) reports that one of the greatest fears most people have is dying alone. Thus, social contact is also an important aspect that should be addressed in end-of-life spiritual care. Examples of such contact may be companionship on the part of family, friends and institutional staff that allow the person to express her fears or reminisce. Social contact can also be fostered in the context of shared activities, such as two people reading or listening to music together.

Unfortunately family members and others who are the source of such social contact are themselves at high risk for psychosocial morbidity and dysfunction following the loss of the palliative care patient. Kissane and colleagues (2002) found a positive relationship between such morbidity and dysfunction among 81 families who were grieving the loss of a palliative care patient. Furthermore, in a screening of 257 additional bereaved families, Kissane et al. reported that nearly three-quarters (71%) were at risk for poor psychosocial outcomes. This highlights the importance of considering family members in the treatment strategy of the palliative care patient, especially in terms of psychosocial and spiritual concerns. Thus, the spiritual concerns of end-of-life care should extend beyond the patient to his or her family members and significant others who must cope with the anticipated loss of the patient, as well as grief and bereavement after the patient has died. The principles of palliative care extend to these significant others, namely the holistic consideration of a person's physical, psychosocial and spiritual needs (Davies et al., 2002).

Spirituality and Psychosocial Well-Being

Henderson and colleagues (2002) examined the physical and psychosocial needs of 259 nursing home palliative care patients during the last three months of life. Primary physical complaints included pain, personal cleanliness, dyspnea, incontinence, and fatigue. While these physical health issues may be inevitable when dealing with terminal illness, Henderson et al. further noted high levels of psychological morbidity in this population; 44% had depressed mood, 31% reported anxiety, and loneliness was a problem for one-fifth of patients. Thus, while there may be little hope for a cure and physical healing, there is still great potential for psychosocial and spiritual healing for the terminally ill patient (Twycross, 2002).

Addressing spiritual needs at the end of life can make the dying process seem more natural for terminally ill patients. For example, Steinhauser et al. (2000) found that for patients at the end of life, coming to peace with God, meeting with a clergy member, and having the chance to talk about the meaning of death and spiritual beliefs were very important. Saunders (1988) indicated that hospitalized patients find personal beliefs and practices important. Furthermore, prayer is often used to cope with stress regardless of income, marital stress, religious affiliation, or age (Dunn & Horgas, 2000).

McClain, Rosenfeld, and Breitbart (2003) examined the effects of spiritual well-being on end-of-life despair among 160 patients in a palliative care hospital with life expectancies of three months or less. The authors found significant negative relationships between spiritual well-being and desire for a quick death, suicidal ideation, and hopelessness. There was also an interesting interaction between spiritual well-being and depression regarding these outcomes, in that high levels of spirituality mitigated the positive relation between depression and desire for a hastened death.

Spirituality has also been found to have a beneficial effect on the bereavement of family members following the death of a loved one. Walsh, King, Jones, Tookman, and Blizard (2002) conducted a prospective study of spirituality and bereavement among 135 friends and relatives of patients with a terminal illness. Levels of grief were assessed one, nine and 14 months following the patient's death. Participants were divided into three spiritual belief groups based on their responses to a spiritual beliefs scale: (a) strong beliefs (above median on scale; $n = 44$), (b) low beliefs (below median on scale; $n = 40$); and (c) no beliefs (score of 0 on scale; $n = 11$). Results found that those individuals with strong spiritual beliefs were able to resolve their grief over the 14-month course of the study, but those with no spiritual beliefs were not able to resolve their grief in this time period. Those with low belief levels appeared to show no change over the first nine months, but subsequently came to resolution of their grief by 14 months. The results of Walsh and colleagues study suggest that the strength of spiritual belief is related to positive grief resolution. Thus, interventions in palliative care settings that support the spiritual beliefs and well-being of the patient's significant others, when such beliefs are present, may be effective in addressing psychosocial morbidity associated with bereavement.

Designing Spiritual Interventions for Palliative Care

Addressing the spiritual well-being of a dying person may help the individual to have a more peaceful end, while at the same time help family and friends cope better with their loss. Palliative care is best delivered in the context of a multidisciplinary team, usually consisting of physicians, nurses, health care aids, and volunteers (Rumbold, 2003; Twycross, 2002). In addition, the specialty of pastoral care has seen a reemergence in health care settings to address the spiritual health and well-being of the patient, including those individuals at the end of life and/or receiving palliative care (Seidl, 1990).

While religious resources have historically been used to address spiritual well-being in palliative care, this has evolved into broader awareness of the idiosyncratic nature of spiritual belief, in that many people today consider themselves to be spiritual without ties to a specific religious denomination (Rumbold, 2003). Thus, it is important for those caring for dying persons not to have preconceived notions about the spirituality of their patients. Spirituality holds different meanings for different people and can be expressed in many ways, from traditional religious practices to "New Age" modalities (e.g., meditation), to practices of a more personal nature. It would be a mistake to think that there is one particular spiritual intervention that could completely serve all dying individuals. Therefore, a dying individual should be able to determine how and when she would like to address her spiritual well-being (Rumbold, 2003).

Hence, providing a range of spiritually enriching options from which a person can choose autonomously and at his discretion may be a better approach than rigid and structured modalities of spiritual intervention. This would allow for the support of private and public spiritual practices as the individual desires. Some examples of these practices range from reading spiritual literature, to listening to soothing nature sounds, consulting or praying with a spiritual advisor, using aromatherapy, or listening to meaningful music with a family member. By having the ability to choose how they would like to address their own spiritual needs, patients avoid some of the well-intentioned, but inappropriate proselytizing that may occur when standard "religious" interventions are put into place. Furthermore, addressing the subjective features of the palliative care patient's personal connections to significant others and important activities can help insure quality of care through a better understanding of the care recipient's individual spiritual needs. These may range from sharing music that has personal significance, to engaging in conversations, reflecting on one's past life, or reading materials of personal significance (e.g., scriptures and other religious texts).

The CARE Cabinet Intervention

The pastoral services department advisory council at a skilled-nursing facility, consisting of an interdisciplinary group of direct care and ancillary service providers, developed the Creating Alternative Relaxing Environment (CARE) Cabinet as an intervention to meet the end-of-life needs of palliative care patients. The program offers a bedside spiritual intervention through the portable CARE Cabinet. The CARE Cabinet was an effort to comfort and support residents, their families and friends in their spiritual needs during the often difficult period near the end of life.

The palliative care team selected items for the CARE Cabinet with the aim of providing beneficial emotional and spiritual wellness, as well as fostering social interaction. Contents of the CARE Cabinet were chosen to facilitate spiritual well-being and included reading materials (i.e., Bibles and other inspirational books or pamphlets), audio (i.e., an AM-FM radio with cassette and CD and a nature sounds machine), and an aromatherapy diffuser. In addition, the Cabinet contained items to encourage visiting and social interaction with the patient, including snacks (e.g., candies) and complimentary tickets for cafeteria meals.

For the present article, the effects of this intervention program addressing the psychosocial and spiritual needs of residents who receive palliative care with a unique emphasis on their spiritual concerns were examined. The project studied whether a spiritual intervention could positively influence the well-being of individuals receiving end-of-life care and their families. Two major research questions were addressed:

1. Did the CARE Cabinet help patients and their families/significant others in meeting their spiritual needs and concerns? If so, how?
2. Did the CARE Cabinet facilitate the level and quality of contact between the resident and family members, friends, or volunteers?

METHOD

Participants

Cases for this paper were obtained from residents receiving palliative care at a skilled nursing facility in the Washington Heights section of New York City. Palliative care is delivered on all 18 units of this 705-bed facility; consequently, there is no separate palliative care ward. The CARE Cabinet was sequentially placed with three residents. One participant was Hispanic, one African American, and one was European American. Two men and one woman received the intervention, and their ages ranged from 47 to 84 years.

The CARE Cabinet

A cabinet was chosen as the container for the CARE intervention by the palliative care team so that the most frequently used items could remain easily accessible on open shelves, while less frequently used items could be stored behind a cabinet door or in a drawer. The cabinet was designed to hold its contents in an organized and neat manner to facilitate the location and use of items by the care recipient. The CARE Cabinet was constructed of dark wood with light wood veneer inlay on the drawer and cabinet door (see Figure 1). It was 113 mm high and 46 mm wide. There were two open shelves without doors on the top of the cabinet. The top shelf measured 17.5 mm high and 41 mm wide. The second

FIGURE 1. The CARE Cabinet in the Room of a Patient Receiving Palliative Care

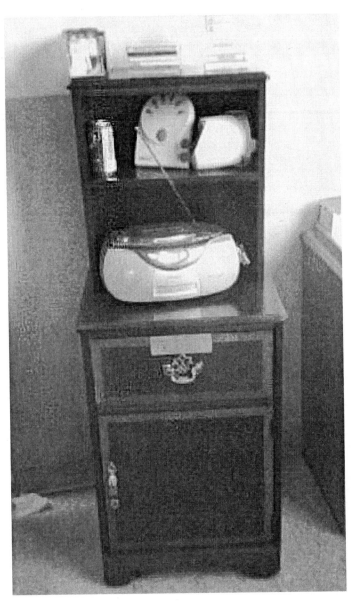

Printed with permission.

shelf measured 24.5 mm high and 41 mm wide. Below the open shelves was a drawer that measured 19 mm high and 44mm wide. The bottom part of the cabinet held two shelves. The third shelf measured 18 mm high and 44 mm wide. The bottom shelf measured 19 mm high and 44 mm wide. This cabinet was portable and could be placed in patient rooms by a single individual.

CARE Cabinet Contents. The palliative care team chose the Cabinet contents based on committee discussions and suggestions from committee members. The top shelf held a *Fan Fuser* (a portable fan for aromatherapy), and a *Homedics* sound machine with options for different sounds (i.e., heartbeat, spring rain, ocean waves, and summer night). The sounds could be played on a timer for 15, 30, and 60 minutes. The second shelf held a *Magnavox MCS200SL* CD boom box with CD, tape, and radio players. In the drawer below the second shelf was a taped compilation of mixed music, 1 CD-ROM of Spanish Poems (i.e., "Poemas de Siempre"), 1 CD-ROM entitled "Golden Slumbers–A Father's Lullaby," a bowl of assorted hard fruit candy, two meal tickets, three individually packaged perfumed freshening hand towels, a description of the CARE cabinet, and four pamphlets (i.e., *Finding Meaning in Suffering, Living with a Problem You Can't Solve, Facing Death with Faith and Courage*, and *Praying with Someone Sick*).

The third shelf held four books including *Celtic Portraits, Poetry Speaks, Life Spectrum*, and *Decade of Triumph–The 40s*. The fourth shelf held a Bible, a New World Translation of the Holy Scripture, a JPS Hebrew English Bible, and a book entitled, *Knowledge That Leads to Everlasting Life*. On the very top of the cabinet were assorted cassette tapes by various artists (i.e., Tommy Dorsey and Frank Sinatra, Louis Armstrong, Benny Goodman, Duke Ellington, Harry James, Glenn Miller, Artie Shaw and Count Basie, Jimmy Dorsey, Bing Crosby, Jo Stafford, Frank Sinatra and Count Basie, Fats Waller, and Ella Fitzgerald). The top of the cabinet could be used to display personal photos provided by the patient.

Intervention Procedures

Prior to the inception of the program, the pastoral services department provided an overview of the CARE Cabinet intervention and an explanation of its use to the 18 unit coordinators at the facility. The unit coordinators were encouraged to make referrals and to help the primary caregivers assist the patients with the items in the cabinet. Members of the multidisciplinary nursing home staff, such as recreation, rehabilitation, social services, physicians, and psychologists, were also asked to make referrals for the CARE Cabinet to the Assistant Director of Nursing. Facility nursing staff was informed of the implementation of this intervention, but did not receive formal training on the use of the CARE Cabinet with palliative care patients. Bedside volunteers from Pastoral Services did receive training on the intervention from pastoral services staff.

The two criteria for potential cabinet care users were: (a) terminal illness (i.e., expected to die within three to six months); and (b) the potential user and/or their visitors must be able to use the contents of the cabinet. If these criteria were met, the Assistant Director of Nursing contacted the Director of Pastoral Services with the new referral. The Director of Pastoral Services made an in-person assessment of all new referrals to evaluate the appropriateness of the intervention for each case, for example, the level of patient awareness, number of visitors, other support received from family and friends, and an initial assessment of what contents the patient would be able to use. For example, if the individual was only able to use one or two items, only those items were given to the individual rather than the whole cabinet. If an individual did not have visitors and was unable to access the items from the cabinet independently, individual items that could be used, such as music or aromatherapy, were left with the patient. The Director of Pastoral services ranked potential candidates in order of need based on the aforementioned criteria for potential users because there was only a single CARE Cabinet available. However, individuals on the waiting list were sometimes given individual items until the cabinet became available.

Once an individual was determined to be a good candidate for the intervention, pastoral services moved the CARE cabinet to the patient's room. At this time someone from the pastoral services staff explained the CARE Cabinet contents to the patient, family, and friends. For example, the Pastoral Director met with the child of one patient who then explained the cabinet and its contents in Spanish to the patient's wife. The CARE Cabinet was left with the patient until he or she died or until it was no longer useful. The Assistant Director of Recreation checked every two to three days to see if anything needed to be replenished and if the contents were being utilized, and restocked the cabinet weekly. The Pastoral Director also met once a month with the volunteers to discuss the use of the cabinet items, determine what the resident and volunteer liked or disliked about the intervention, and determine if new items were needed (e.g., replenish snacks or meal tickets).

Design and Qualitative Analysis

The evaluation of this project uses a case study design to examine the effectiveness of the CARE Cabinet intervention for palliative care patients in this pilot project. Narrative accounts provided by the Director of Pastoral Services, other staff, and volunteers involved with the three cases provided evidence for the effectiveness of the intervention. In order to address the research questions concerning whether or not the CARE Cabinet facilitated spiritual well-being among care recipients as well as how the intervention may have enhanced opportunities for social interaction between the patient, family and friends, and volunteers, these narratives were composed into three case studies, and were subjected to qualitative content analysis.

RESULTS

The following case studies are based on the three initial palliative care patients who consented to the CARE Cabinet intervention. Personal information about these cases has been changed to preserve patient anonymity, but other information in the case studies reflects the actual implementation of the intervention.

Case Study Number One

Mr. A., a Spanish-speaking 47-year-old man who suffered from a terminal illness, was expected to live no longer than three to six months. He had a very supportive family. His wife and son, the family members involved with him, took turns staying with him around the clock, even sleeping on the floor. They felt he should never be left alone. He did not have volunteers because his family was very involved with his care and wanted to spend as much time with him as possible. This family utilized the CARE Cabinet every day in shared activities with the patient and by themselves as described below.

The CARE Cabinet was able to support the spiritual needs and practices of the patient and his family in a number of ways. The patient enjoyed listening to music and using the aromatherapy diffuser; such experiences may have helped him to transcend the immediate circumstances of his terminal illness. His wife, who believed in reading the scripture for comfort, read the Spanish language Bible each day. The comfort she received from reading Scripture helped her to cope with the impending loss of her husband. In fact, the resident's wife enjoyed the Bible to such a degree that she took it home with her after the death of her husband. This allowed her to keep a positive reminder of her husband and her experience with him at the end of his life. She was thus able to take with her a physical reminder of her experience that she could continue to use and have as a connection to her departed spouse.

Additionally, the family members were able to pursue their own spiritual comfort autonomously while remaining physically present in the room and keeping company with the patient. The wife and son reported that they listened to the nature sounds, used the aroma diffuser, and the radio with the pillow speaker. They also enjoyed listening to Spanish music together. This helped them to spend time together, while still pursuing their individual needs for comfort. The family members also used the cabinet to store personal items, such as sleepwear and socks, so they could rest comfortably in a more home-like environment while visiting with the patient.

The CARE Cabinet also helped to maintain the connections between this patient and his family at the end of life, which are vital to both psychological and spiritual well-being. The family members ate the candy and used the meal tickets so they could eat in the cafeteria rather than go home for meals (see Table 1). Thus, The CARE cabinet helped the family to feel like they were not abandoning their father and husband, because they were able to stay with him round the clock.

Mr. A. kept the CARE cabinet until his death. The CARE Cabinet had a profound effect on this family in supporting their spiritual needs and well-being. The intervention facilitated their ability to engage in both shared and solitary activities that allowed them to reflect, think, and pursue spiritual well-being. The CARE Cabinet also supported the maintenance of social connections between this patient and his family during the last weeks of his life.

Case Study Number Two

Mrs. B. was an 84-year-old widow with dementia and depression. She was dying of congestive heart failure and was expected to live no longer than six months. She had declined psychological services for depression, and required extensive assistance from staff for her Activities of Daily Living (ADLs). She did not have any family, but had a pastoral services volunteer who visited regularly. She also had visitation from pastoral services approximately four times per week. These visits in-

TABLE 1. Chart of CARE Cabinet Items Used by Patients Receiving Palliative Care

CARE Cabinet Item	Mr. A	Mrs. B	Mr. C
Aromatherapy	X		
Nature Sounds	X	X	
CD/Tape/Radio Player	X	X	X
Tapes in English and Spanish			X
CD-ROMs in English and Spanish	X	X	X
Candy	X		
Meal Tickets	X		
Perfumed Hand Towels			
Spiritual Pamphlets		X	
Books		X	
Bibles	X		

cluded prayer, visiting, reading, and/or utilizing items from the CARE Cabinet (see Table 1).

The volunteer and the patient used items from the CARE cabinet together approximately four times weekly; the sound machine, radio, CD/cassette, and reading materials were the most popular. In the case of Mrs. B., the CARE Cabinet facilitated her spiritual well-being by helping her to address unresolved life issues and find purpose and meaning in life. The volunteer told us the resident had issues "she wanted to get off her chest." The volunteer was able to use the materials in the CARE Cabinet to start a life review process with the patient. The volunteer mentioned that she played the nature sounds for the patient, and her favorite was the summer sounds of crickets, which helped her to relax, become less agitated and fall asleep. The volunteer believed that the summer sounds of crickets reminded the patient of her home and growing up down south.

The volunteer also spent time with the patient listening to jazz CDs, such as Ella Fitzgerald. The patient had reported that she listened to Ella Fitzgerald when she was young, and she reminisced about her move from down south to New York City as a young woman. The patient preferred the CDs to the radio because she found it difficult to find a station that played music from the era when she was growing up. Thus, she was able to choose a CD she liked, and she was surprised and pleased that she was able to listen to exactly what she wanted. Prior to the introduction of the CARE Cabinet and CD player, Mrs. B. didn't care for music on the radio, and didn't spend much time listening to it because the music on the radio did not provide the connection to her past that she was seeking. Thus, the CD music and nature sounds from the CARE cabinet helped Mrs. B. talk about her past and helped her to reminisce about her family, all of whom were dead. By going through the process of reminiscence or life review, Mrs. B. was able to reconnect with her youth as she faced the end of her life.

The CARE Cabinet also helped to foster social contact with Mrs. B., despite the absence of family members. She did not have a television, and was virtually without stimulation other than that from visitors. The volunteer stated that the items in the cabinet, particularly the CDs, enabled her to visit longer with the resident because they were both interested in listening to the music. In fact, the volunteer stayed as long as two hours at a time with the resident. Thus, the CARE Cabinet helped Mrs. B. to have stimulation and memories that helped her not to feel alone at the end of life. This patient kept the CARE cabinet until her death.

This volunteer thought the cabinet was useful and helpful to this resident. In fact, she stated the CARE Cabinet "was a positive thing for her." This volunteer was very enthusiastic about the CARE cabinet as a tool for helping her to become closer to the resident. Additionally, the volunteer suggested more publicity, training, and awareness for all staff members be undertaken so that anyone in the facility could turn on the radio for the resident, or help a resident access the materials while doing their jobs. She also suggested putting a tape recorder in the cabinet to help facilitate a life review process with dying residents, so that the tape could be given to family members after the patient had died.

Case Study Number Three

Mr. C. was a 78-year-old divorced man who suffered from depression and multiple medical conditions. He was terminally ill and expected to live no longer than six months. He required extensive assistance from staff for ADLs. He was without family to provide support, but he did have a pastoral services volunteer who visited regularly. He had been receiving psychological services for depression and received visitations from the pastoral services staff four days per week. These visits included prayer, visiting, reading, and/or utilizing items from the CARE cabinet (see Table 1). The CARE Cabinet offered the resident and his volunteer a variety of ways to facilitate their social interaction and help create a more comfortable and nurturing environment for the patient.

Similar to the preceding case, the CARE Cabinet allowed Mr. C. to connect to his past by listening to music that was special to him. The volunteer stated the CARE Cabinet was "a Godsend," because the resident liked music, had been a singer in his earlier years, and enjoyed talking about music. The volunteer continued, "It's made such a difference in the last couple of months." The music helped the patient to reminisce with the volunteer during their meetings. The volunteer even brought in Big Band music the resident requested such as Tommy Dorsey, Bing Crosby, and Frank Sinatra, which the volunteer left in the cabinet for the resident to use when he was not visiting.

As he neared the end of his life, Mr. C. was declining and rarely able to respond to individuals except when meeting with his volunteer. The volunteer requested that Mr. C. be able to keep the CARE Cabinet until his death. Even during the final days of his life, the CARE Cabinet continued to be a benefit to Mr. C. because he could listen to his music while alone or with others. Thus, listening to music facilitated social interaction between the patient and volunteers, which was crucial given his limited social support resources. He was able to listen to music that made him feel relaxed and brought him pleasure, and helped him to reminisce about his past. The CARE cabinet allowed Mr. C. to nurture his spiritual well-being both autonomously and in the company of others.

DISCUSSION

The CARE Cabinet Intervention was designed as an intervention to meet the spiritual and psychosocial needs of palliative care patients. Items included in the Cabinet were intended to facilitate emotional well-ness and spiritual well-being, in addition to promoting both brief and extended social contact with family, friends, and volunteer caregivers. The case studies presented here have shown that this spiritual intervention has made a positive impact on the patients and family members who participated. Based on these findings, making the CARE Cabinet available to patients receiving palliative care would be worthwhile and beneficial to both patients and family members. Other staff members at this facility share this view. For example, a staff psychologist recently requested a component of the CARE Cabinet for a resident whose end of life was made more comforting by playing music on demand "that spoke to her spirit."

Based on anecdotal descriptions made by the pastoral services department, recreation department, and the volunteers, the three case studies described above provided evidence that the contents of the CARE Cabinet were used as intended. Family involvement was facilitated through shared use of cabinet contents and supportive items placed in the cabinet (e.g., meal tickets, candy). The types of materials used varied by the needs and interests of the patient and their family members (see Table 1). For example, only Mr. A. and his family used the candy and meal tickets. These CARE Cabinet items enabled the family to stay with Mr. A. around the clock, as they desired. In the cases of Mrs. B. and Mr. C., who lacked social support other than volunteers, these items were not used. Mr. A. and his family took comfort in reading the Bible, while Mrs. B. preferred other types of spiritual books and pamphlets. All three cases utilized the audio players, but only Mr. A. and Mrs. B. took advantage of the nature sounds machine, and only Mr. A. used the aromatherapy device. These case reports illustrate the idiosyncratic nature of the spiritual and psychosocial needs of patients and their families in palliative care settings, and support the decision to make this an "open" intervention in the sense of allowing patients to choose those items that best meet their needs.

As noted previously, some of the greatest fears at the end of life involve dying alone and abandonment (National Cancer Institute, 2002), and as Henderson and colleagues (2002) noted, anxiety and loneliness are two of the major psychological issues in this population. In all three of the case studies reported earlier, the CARE Cabinet was effective in increasing social contact between the patient and family members and volunteers. For example, in the case of Mr. A., his involved and caring family was able to spend more time with him since meal tickets were provided, and they did not have to leave the facility to take meals. The Spanish music also served as a basis for interaction between Mr. A. and his family. In the case of Mrs. B., who had no family available, the CARE Cabinet contents promoted interactions between her and the pastoral services volunteer, including listening to music, reading together, and even engaging in a life review to resolve outstanding issues from her life. Mr. C., who also lacked family members, also benefitted from increased social interaction with his volunteer due to the CARE Cabinet contents, as demonstrated by the active involvement of the volunteer in obtaining music Mr. C. enjoyed. Thus, the CARE Cabinet intervention had a positive effect on social interactions in the three case studies presented in this article.

Practice and Research Implications

Based on the growing waiting list for CARE Cabinets for residents receiving palliative care (i.e., approximately 50 at the time of this writing), and the positive feedback from patients, families, and volunteers who have used the CARE Cabinet, the palliative care committee intends to purchase additional CARE Cabinets to make this intervention more widely available. While there were no apparent barriers or resistance to the implementation of this intervention on the part of nursing and other staff, the narratives we received concerning this intervention suggested staff involvement with the CARE Cabinet, other than pastoral services volunteers, was minimal. This could likely be remedied by implementing a formal training program on the CARE Cabinet and its use with such staff, which would make them more knowledgeable about the program and may encourage greater involvement from staff in future applications.

Based on the authors' conversations with the institutional staff and volunteers, some additional suggestions for future applications of this intervention are proposed:

- A tape recorder in the cabinet with blank tapes to be used for life review, thoughts and inspirations, or words from the resident.
- Audio tapes/CD's of books in English and in Spanish.
- Frequent contact with family members and volunteers to determine individual needs of the patient and family members, and volunteers using the cabinet.
- Customizing Cabinet contents by providing content (i.e., CDs, books) that is requested on an individual basis to make the materials more meaningful.

As this program is expanded, it should receive systematic evaluation for its effectiveness in meeting the spiritual needs of residents. Such an evaluation should ascertain how this intervention addresses the spiritual well-being and social interaction needs of patients and their families, staff and volunteers through the use of formal assessments administered regularly during the intervention episode and following the death of the patient. This would provide evidence to aid in the continued improvement of this intervention, and help support efforts to make the CARE Cabinet available to all palliative care patients.

Future application and evaluation of this intervention should be undertaken at other facilities in order to examine the generalizability to other populations. Furthermore, this intervention could be expanded beyond the palliative care setting to all residents in long-term care facilities to address their spiritual concerns in later life and facilitate social interaction. While this study is limited in generalizability due to the case study methodology employed in this pilot project, the results appear to be generally positive and warrant further application and evaluation. The present findings do affirm our research questions concerning whether or not this intervention has helped these individuals and their significant others to nurture their spiritual selves as well as to support the other significant relationships in their lives.

REFERENCES

Davies, B., Brenner, P., Orloff, S., Sumner, L., & Worden, W. (2002). Addressing spirituality in pediatric hospice and palliative care. *Journal of Palliative Care, 18* (1), 59-67.

Dunn, K. S., & Horgas, A. L. (2000). The prevalence of prayer as a spiritual self-care modality in elders. *Journal of Holistic Nursing, 18* (4), 337-351.

Ersek, M., & Wilson, S. A. (2003). The challenges and opportunities in providing end-of-life care in nursing homes. *Journal of Palliative Medicine, 6* (1), 45-57.

Kissane, D. W., McKenzie, M., McKenzie, D. P., Forbes, A., O'Neill, I., & Bloch, S. (2003). Psychosocial morbidity associated with patterns of family functioning in palliative care: Baseline data from the Family Focused Grief Therapy controlled trial. *Palliative Medicine, 17* (6), 527-37.

McClain, C. S., Rosenfeld, B., & Breitbart, W. (2003). Effect of spiritual well-being on end-of-life despair in terminally ill cancer patients. *Lancet, 10: 361* (9369), 1603-7.

National Cancer Insititute (2002). Retrieved from the World Wide Web September 9, 2003 from: *http://cis.nci.nih.gov/fact/8_15.htm.*

Perron, V., & Schonwetter, R. (2001). Hospice and palliative care programs. *Primary Care, 28* (2), 427-440.

Reynolds, K., Henderson, M., Schulman, A., & Hanson, L. C. (2002). Needs of the dying in nursing homes. *Journal of Palliative Medicine, 5* (6), 895-901.

Rumbold, B. D. (2003). Caring for the spirit: Lessons from working with the dying. *Medical Journal of Australia, 179* (6), S11-13.

Saunders, D. C. (1988). Forum-Spiritual Pain. *Journal of Palliative Care, 4* (3), 29-32.

Seidl, L. G. (1990). The renaissance of pastoral care. *Health Progress, 71* (2), 58-60.

Steinhauser, K. E., Christakis, N. A., Clipp, E. C., McNeilly, M., McIntyre, L., & Tulsky, J. A. (2000). Factors considered important at the end of life by patients, family, physicians, and other care providers. *Journal of the American Medical Association (JAMA), 284* (19), 2476-2482.

Sulmasy, D. P. (2002). A biopsychosocial-spiritual model for the care of patients at the end of life. *The Gerontologist*, 42, 24-33.

Twycross, R. G. (2002). The challenge of palliative care. *International Journal of Clinical Oncology, 7* (4), 271-278.

Walsh, K., King, M., Jones, L., Tookman, A., & Blizard, R. (2002). Spiritual beliefs may affect outcome of bereavement: Prospective study. *British Medical Journal, 29: 324* (7353), 1551.

Spiritual Caregiving
for Older Adults:
A Perspective
from Clinical Practice

Ralph DePalo, PhD
Mark Brennan, PhD

SUMMARY. Spiritual care has been described as being holistic and cutting across professional disciplines. By taking a transdisciplinary approach, all health and social service providers have the potential for providing spiritual comfort to their patients, clients, and consumers. Spiritual assessment allows the clinician to obtain a deeper knowledge of the individual's strengths, weaknesses and coping style. Implementing a spiritual intervention imbues clinical practice with a sense of vitality, creativity, movement, and reaching out to make significant connections with others. Thus, one of the main charges of spiritual caregiving is to be available and present when patients and clients face the unknown and unknowable. As clinicians begin to speak to the multi-

Ralph DePalo is Intake Manager, CCM/P.A.C.E. Program, Beth Abraham Health Services, 375 Grand Street, New York, NY 10002 (E-mail: RDepalo@bethabe.org). Dr. DePalo is also Adjunct Professor at New York University. Mark Brennan is Senior Research Associate, Lighthouse International, 111 East 59th Street, New York, NY 10022-1202 (E-mail: mbrennan@lighthouse.org).

[Haworth co-indexing entry note]: "Spiritual Caregiving for Older Adults: A Perspective from Clinical Practice." DePalo, Ralph, and Mark Brennan. Co-published simultaneously in *Journal of Religion, Spirituality & Aging* (The Haworth Pastoral Press, an imprint of The Haworth Press, Inc.) Vol. 17, No. 1/2, 2004, pp. 151-160; and: *Spiritual Assessment and Intervention with Older Adults: Current Directions and Applications* (ed: Mark Brennan, and Deborah Heiser) The Haworth Pastoral Press, an imprint of The Haworth Press, Inc., 2004, pp. 151-160. Single or multiple copies of this article are available for a fee from The Haworth Document Delivery Service [1-800-HAWORTH, 9:00 a.m. - 5:00 p.m. (EST). E-mail address: docdelivery@haworthpress.com].

Digital Object Identifier: 10.1300/J496v17n01_08

tude of biopsychosocial and cultural factors relevant to the spiritual well-being of older adults there must be clinical guidelines. However, given the relatively recent attention to spiritual intervention, such guidelines are lacking and should be developed in the near future. However, clinicians may become catalysts in helping individuals to achieve a measure of calming fulfillment and spiritual well-being as they face the challenges of later life. *[Article copies available for a fee from The Haworth Document Delivery Service: 1-800-HAWORTH. E-mail address: <docdelivery@ haworthpress.com> Website: <http://www.HaworthPress.com> © 2004 by The Haworth Press, Inc. All rights reserved.]*

KEYWORDS. Clinical practice, transdisciplinary, spiritual well-being, spiritual caregiving

Theorists have long believed that religiousness and spirituality are appropriate topics for both clinical practice and for scientific research (Moberg, 1971, 1979, 1986, 2002; Howden, 1989, 1992; Pargament, 1997). The growing number of scientific investigations on this topic suggests a surge of interest in spirituality and spiritual well-being. The research on spiritual assessment and intervention presented in this volume clearly suggests that spirituality and spiritual caregiving are both a necessary requirement and vital nutriment in the holistic care of older adults. What, then, are the practice implications of the conceptual and empirical work on spiritual assessment and intervention?

Spiritual Challenges for Clinical Practice

Therapists have considered the value and practical applications of religion, religious impulses, and the yearning for transcendent experiences as basic human needs and pathways to emotional wholeness (Moberg, 1971; Hart, 1989; Goldman, 1991). Spiritual care has been described as being holistic and cutting across professional disciplines, and Pruyser (1976a) notes that professionals from a wide variety of backgrounds can incorporate spirituality in their work, just as other factors relevant to the human condition (i.e., growing old, suffering, pleasures, morality) also have an impact on their work. Pruyser further notes that such a transdisciplinary approach will give such work on spiritual issues a unique stamp depending upon the particular discipline. Given the explosion of empirical work documenting the generally positive effects of spirituality on physical and mental health, clinicians are currently faced with the challenge, as well as the opportunity, to engage spiritual concerns, to strengthen them, and to therapeutically use spirituality in work with older adults regardless of our particular professional discipline.

In taking such a transdisciplinary approach, all health and social service providers have the potential for providing spiritual comfort to their patients, clients, and consumers (Stitt, 1952). Cornett (1992) admonishes those of us in clinical practice not to overlook the spiritual well-being of the client who may be seeking assistance; ". . . the failure to integrate spirituality into our clinical thinking represents an impoverishment . . . unfortunately, we also often diminish the tremendous growth that our clients could achieve through exploration of the spiritual aspects of their lives . . ." (p. 101). Cornett goes on to advocate for a "biopsychosocial-spiritual model of human functioning" that legitimatizes the recognition of spiritual issues in clinical practice, and provides the clinician with a more complete picture of the client's problems, challenges, and resources. Furthermore, the older adult, their family and their significant others may suffer from diminished spiritual well-being due to the failure of service providers to integrate and conceptualize the importance of spirituality in their practice (Hay, 1989).

Spiritual Concerns in Clinical Practice

There are notable characteristics of spirituality that account for its role in the development of human beings. The scope of these spiritual concerns encompasses inner resources and transcendence, connections to others in the community, and life's purpose and meaning (Howden, 1992). First, spirituality results in an enhancement of one's own inner resources, namely, supporting hope in the face of the challenges of life and allowing one to transcend difficulties by adopting a more spiritual perspective on life experience. Secondly, spirituality occurs in the context of communities of which one is a part. While spirituality may be expressed in idiosyncratic and private ways, for most people, spirituality involves connections to the community whether in the form of membership and participation in a religious congregation (Pargament, 1997), or to the extent that one's spiritual grounding influences our relationships with others. Finally, spirituality infuses purpose and meaning to life, providing a lens through which events and circumstances are experienced, assessed, and acted upon. These aforementioned domains are congruent with the definition of spiritual suffering and pain as entities that bridge the gap between individual and community experience, but result in interpersonal and interpsychic distress (Hay, 1989).

SPIRITUAL CAREGIVING IN CLINICAL PRACTICE

Attention to spiritual well-being and spiritual caregiving are necessary requirements when providing holistic care for the older adult (Bell, 1985; Hiatt, 1986; Stitt, 1952). Spiritual well-being, fostered through spiritual caregiving, acts as "the glue" in the maintenance of a patient's or client's sense of personal integrity, providing an intersubjective sense of identity, continuity and self-determination. Furthermore, the goal of the practitioner in providing holistic care is to create an atmosphere of comfort, support, hope and strength allowing both the continuance as well as the formation of new, healthy and secure emotional bonds between the client and significant others. These emotional bonds are important when addressing concerns of human experience, which can include gains and losses, joy and suffering, and life and death.

The Importance of Spiritual Assessment

Understanding the spiritual well-being and needs of older adults allows the clinician to obtain a deeper knowledge of the individual's strengths, weaknesses and coping style. The practitioner achieves this deeper understanding of the intersubjective domains of the client, including that of spirituality, through clinical assessment of the individual, family, group, and in some instance, the community. It is through this process that the clinician has the opportunity to develop a therapeutic alliance with the client when addressing spiritual pain and suffering. This therapeutic alliance is the vehicle through which the dynamics, creativity and movement of spiritual resources and well-being are defined and addressed.

In order to establish a valid therapeutic alliance, it is most crucial that clinicians not impose their own values, beliefs and norms. Instead, the practitioner should embrace the cultural nuances of the older adult including those that are relevant to spirituality. Along these lines and as an adjunct to clinical assessment, it is paramount that a comprehensive self-assessment be obtained from the older adult client. Such a self-assessment supports clinical values of self-determination and empowerment on the part of the client. Additionally, self-assessment strengthens the bond of trust between the clinician and the older adult because it helps the clinician to develop an individualized and tailored treatment plan that is germane to the cultural and spiritual constitution and concerns of the older adult.

The importance of obtaining spiritual self-assessment is supported by the idea that in order to understand clients on their own terms, the clinician must demonstrate a commitment to the therapeutic relationship and stay as close as possible to what the clients relate about their own experience. DeYoung (2003) describes this type of rapport as relational therapy, which is all about "self with other" (p. 1). DeYoung also remarks that both the client and practitioner possess characteristics of humanness and vulnerability, and both parties must address these issues through candidness, fortitude and in a spirit of good faith. Thus, in the context of assessment and the provision of spiritual care, fundamentals of clinical practice, namely, positive regard, empathy, respect and humaneness are important throughout the therapeutic relationship from initial assessment until case closure.

The Dynamics of Spiritual Intervention in Practice

There is a sense of vitality, creativity, movement, and reaching out when implementing a spiritual intervention. As Conrad (1985) aptly notes, any caring relationship will automatically include spiritual support. In many instances, the provision of spiritual support does not involve anything beyond practitioners being available and present for their clients as they negotiate the vagaries and challenges of later life. As articulated by Saunders and Baines (1983):

> Whoever we are and whatever our beliefs, we may have to face questions from our patients and their families that we are unable to answer. . . . However, it is important we find the strength to listen when we feel we have no answers to give. The command "watch with me" did not mean "take this crisis away," it could not have meant "explain it." The simple yet costly demand was "stay there and stay awake." More of those who try to do this than will perhaps care to admit will find themselves trusting in the Presence that can more easily reach the patient and his family if they themselves concentrate on using all their competence with compassion and say little to interrupt. (p. 64)

Thus, according to Saunders and Baines (1983), one of the main charges of spiritual caregiving is to be available and present when patients and clients face the unknown and unknowable, creating a mutuality in terms of shared experience through such expectant waiting. It is this mutuality that may be the secret of our continued hope, and when absent, leads to hopelessness and despondence. Spiritual interventions enable a "working through" process when identifying feelings of abandonment and loss into a community of hope between the practitioner and the older adult. This allows the older adult to feel nourished by the clinician and diminish the challenges and stresses of events or situations, thus empowering and strengthening the older adult's spiritual well-being.

HOPE AND SPIRITUAL INTERVENTION

Bruhn (1984) acknowledges the therapeutic value of hope and describes it as one way that people cope with both anticipated and actual loss. The chronic illnesses and losses in physical functioning which become more and more likely with increased age can easily lead one to embrace despair; when hope is gone, despair its antithesis, remains. The physical reality of disease, incapacity and loss must be surmounted by the sense of hope so that individuals can set reasonable and attainable goals. Hope, therefore, represents a crucial outcome of spiritual well-being in older adults, and may be engendered through spiritual mechanisms of reliance on inner resources, connectedness to others, and the ability to transcend the physical realities through spiritual beliefs and values.

Hope is endemic to human experience. Hope engenders the possibility that a good future is possible. Although hope and its fruits are intangible, hope reaffirms the vitality of life even in the face of death. When faced with an uncertain future, hope may serve as the basis of future realities, both real and imagined, for in the face of such uncertainty it is hope and all it encompasses that provides a sense of stability. This makes hope a genuine touchstone for existence, for to hope is to acknowledge the future. Because of its intrinsic connection to the future, hope is clearly a product of spirituality. Mudd (1981) states, ". . . without hope we can exist and plod away, but in a hollow and somewhat-robot-like manner. We need hope to connect us to the tree of life" (p. 5).

Hope is essential for more than just physical and psychological well-being. Epperly (1983) postulates that not only does hope support the ability of the body to recuperate, but the maintenance of hope addresses spiritual needs and spiritual well-being. When hope is shattered, there are three major consequent behaviors that have been identified by Fromm (1968). In the first case, those who lose hope resign themselves to fate. While these people may have had average levels of optimism before their crisis, they lose their capacity to dream when they lose their capacity to hope. The second group reacts to loss of hope through opting for isolation as a protection against the profound hurt of unfulfilled hope. For the third group, loss of hope may result in a propensity for self-destructive behavior since the energy once directed toward hopeful goals has no other positive channel.

The Intersection of Hope and Despair

Stoll (1979) stresses that setting unrealistic goals, such as a cure or the cessation of pain and discomfort in the context of chronic or terminal illness, may lead to nothing but "doubt and disillusionment" (p. 1575). However, it is ironic that to have hope, one must first have a sense of its opposite, namely, despair. Vaillot (1970) remarks:

> . . . there is no hope, unless the temptation of despair is possible and without hope, one is left with despair and hopelessness. The individual who hopes uses . . . this tension which could reach the breaking point, in order to grow into being. (p. 271)

Thus, the juxtaposition of hope and despair is the key to appreciating and fighting for one's existence. And hope itself is not one-dimensional, for hope does not stop at one's desired external reality but reaches into one's innermost being. Thus hope has characteristics of both the concrete and abstract (Conrad, 1985; Dufault, 1981).

Lynch (1965) characterizes hope as an internal representation that there is "outside" help to speak to our condition. Lynch goes on to say that the acceptance of this outside help, which forms the foundation of hope, is an inner-directed appropriation of resources that in no way depersonalizes or diminishes the recipient. Lynch further states that hope speaks not only to our futures, but also to our present circumstances. According to this author, hope that is not realistic precludes the experience of mutuality in the present. This is in line with Stoll (1979) who posited that hope must be based in reality so that clients can work through and accept their current situations to retain a sense of life's purpose and meaning for the present and the future.

Hope and the Maintenance of Spiritually Nurturing Mutuality

Another facet worth exploring is the communal instinct of hope. It is the presence of this mutuality that is the secret of all our hopes and it is the absence of this mutuality that makes us hopeless and despondent. The experience of mutuality transforms our dread of abandonment and our terrors of isolation into communities of hope. This type of hope affirms and asserts hope's spiritual nature. Anderson (1989) states, "The kind of mutuality that generates hope includes but transcends hopelessness. It creates an environment in which we are held, in which our pain is held, in which the life-long human need for attachment is maintained and nourished" (p. 148).

Similarly, each professional discipline has its own way of creating this vital mutuality, whether it is through "empathy," a "holding environment," the "therapeutic alliance," and exploring client's transitional objects. The language one uses when discussing hope captures the implicit mutuality and sharing it involves. According to Pruyser (1976b) the way we talk about hope is revealing. That is, hope involves dynamics around relationships, rather than action per se. Hope may be given, received, and in some instances lost. This dynamic captures the essence of hope that is grounded in shared experience with others, and that enhances the mutuality of hope in the context of spiritual caregiving.

CONCLUSIONS AND RECOMMENDATIONS

The findings reported in this volume on spiritual assessment and interventions have immediate relevance for clinical practice and scientific research. The incorporation of a biopsychosocial-spiritual model of human functioning in practice settings should include an assessment of the spiritual and cultural nuances of patients and clients. Providing the client with a self-assessment of what spirituality means to them is highly recommended. These activities would provide a spiritual needs-assessment which would assist practitioners in developing a transdisciplinary treatment care plan that would benefit the client, their family and their significant others.

Through clinical intervention, the practitioner is able to foster and strengthen the older adult's spiritual well-being for a more productive and fruitful life journey. To date, standard treatment modalities have involved individual and group work that enables the older adult to process life experiences and concerns. But, spiritual wellness is not usually addressed. As clinicians begin to speak to the multitude of biopsychosocial and cultural factors relevant to the spiritual well-being of older adults there must be clinical guidelines. However, given the relatively recent attention to spiritual intervention, such guidelines are lacking and need to be developed in the near future.

Although research has shown that spirituality has a direct link to the older adult's wellness (Miller & Thoresen, 2003), future research on spiritual assessment and intervention should explore the validity of these approaches in terms of gender, religious, cultural and socioeconomic variability. Practitioners should be especially concerned with the generalizability of research on spiritual assessment and intervention, since what works in a particular setting with a particular client may not foster the mutuality of a therapeutic relationship that should be present in this type of work. Additionally, it is through these alternative therapeutic connections with older adults that the practitioner has the opportunity to utilize different forms of spiritual treatment modalities. The clinician is challenged to provide the older adult with treatment modalities that will decrease this despondency and instill realistic feelings of hope, and at times may need to consider "nontraditional" approaches. Such modalities may include the use of meditation, guided imagery, music therapy, color therapy, pet therapy and aromatherapy, etc. Finally, the clinician dealing with older adults must strive to create an atmosphere of trust and openness. In this way, the clinician becomes a catalyst in assisting the older adult to achieve a measure of calming fulfillment and spiritual well-being.

REFERENCES

Anderson, H. (1989). After the diagnosis: An operational theology for the terminally ill. *Journal of Pastoral Care, 43* (2), 141-150.

Bell, H. K. (1985). The spiritual care component of palliative care. *Seminars in Oncology, 12*, 482-48.

Bruhn, J. (1984). Therapeutic value of hope. *Southern Medical Journal, 77*, 215-219.

Conrad, N. L. (1985). Spiritual support for the dying. *The Nursing Clinics of North America, 20* (2), 415-420.

Cornett, C. (1992). Toward a more comprehensive personalogy: Integrating a spiritual perspective into social work practice. *Social Work, 37* (2), 101-102.

De Young, P. (2003). *Relational psychotherapy a primer.* New York: Brunner-Routledge.

Dufault, K. J. (1981). *Hope of elderly persons with cancer.* Unpublished doctoral dissertation. Case Western Reserve University, Ann Arbor, Michigan.

Epperly, J. (1983). The cell and the celestial: Spiritual needs of cancer patients. *Journal of the Medical Association of Georgia, 72,* 374-376.

Fromm, E. (1968). *The revolution of hope-toward a humanized technology.* New York: Harper and Row.

Goldman, D. (September 10, 1991). Many therapists now view religious belief as aid, not illusion. *The New York Times: Science Times,* C1, C8.

Hart, Thomas. (1989). Counseling's spiritual dimension: Nine guiding principles. *Journal of Pastoral Care* (43) 2, 111-118.

Hay, M. (1989) Principles of building spiritual assessment tools. *The American Journal of Hospice Care, 6* (5), 25-31.

Hiatt, J. (1986) Spirituality, medicine, and healing. *Southern Medical Journal, 79,* 1736-1737.

Howden, J. (1989). *Spirituality: Concept analysis, synthesis, and derivation.* Unpublished manuscript. Denton, Texas: Texas Women's University.

Howden, J. (1992). *Development and psychometric characteristics of the spirituality assessment scale.* Unpublished doctoral dissertation. Denton, Texas: Texas Women's University.

Lynch, J. J. (1977). *The broken heart: The medical consequences of loneliness.* New York: Basic Books.

Lynch, W. F. (1965). *Images of hope.* New York: Harper and Row.

Miller, W. R., & Thoresen, C. E. (2003). Spirituality, religion, and health. *American Psychologist, 58,* 24-35.

Moberg, D. O. (1971). Spiritual well-being: Background and issues of the technical committee on spiritual well-being. *White House Conference on Aging.* Washington, DC: US Government Printing Office.

Moberg, D. O. (1979). *Spiritual well being: Sociological perspectives.* Washington, DC: University of America Press.

Moberg, D. O. (1986). Spirituality and Science. *Journal of the American Scientific Affiliation, 38* (3) 186-194.

Moberg, D. O. (2002). Assessing and measuring spirituality: Confronting the dilemmas of universal and particular evaluative criteria. *Journal of Adult Development, 9* (1), 47-60.

Mudd, E. R. (1981). Spiritual needs of terminally ill patients. *Bulletin of the American Protestant Hospital Association, 45,* 1-5.

Pargament, K. I. (1997). *The psychology of religion and coping.* New York: Guilford Press.

Pruyser, P. (1976a). *The minister as diagnostician.* Philadelphia: Westminister Press.

Pruyser, P. (1976b). Phenomenology and dynamics of hoping. *Pastoral Psychology, 25* (1), 43.

Saunders, C., & Baines, M. (1983). *Living with dying: The management of terminal disease.* New York: Oxford University Press.

Stitt, P. G. (1952). Teaming together for the whole patient. *Journal of Pastoral Care, 6* (3), 1-10.

Stoll, R. I. (1979). Guidelines for spiritual assessment. *American Journal of Nursing, 82* (12), 42-45.

Vaillot, M. (1970). Hope: An invitation to live. *American Journal of Nursing, 70* (2), 268-275.

Index

BOOK ORDER FORM!

Order a copy of this book with this form or online at:
http://www.haworthpress.com/store/product.asp?sku=5498

Spiritual Assessment and Intervention with Older Adults
Current Directions and Applications

_____ in softbound at $24.95 ISBN-13: 978-0-7890-2748-1. / ISBN-10: 0-7890-2748-8.
_____ in hardbound at $39.95 ISBN-13: 978-0-7890-2747-4. / ISBN-10: 0-7890-2747-X.

COST OF BOOKS _____

POSTAGE & HANDLING _____
US: $4.00 for first book & $1.50
for each additional book.
Outside US: $5.00 for first book
& $2.00 for each additional book.

SUBTOTAL _____

In Canada: add 7% GST. _____

STATE TAX _____
CA, IL, IN, MN, NJ, NY, OH, PA & SD residents
please add appropriate local sales tax.

FINAL TOTAL _____
If paying in Canadian funds, convert
using the current exchange rate,
UNESCO coupons welcome.

❑ BILL ME LATER:
Bill-me option is good on US/Canada/
Mexico orders only; not good to jobbers,
wholesalers, or subscription agencies.

❑ Signature _____

❑ Payment Enclosed: $ _____

❑ PLEASE CHARGE TO MY CREDIT CARD:
❑ Visa ❑ MasterCard ❑ AmEx ❑ Discover
❑ Diner's Club ❑ Eurocard ❑ JCB

Account # _____

Exp Date _____

Signature _____
(Prices in US dollars and subject to change without notice.)

PLEASE PRINT ALL INFORMATION OR ATTACH YOUR BUSINESS CARD

Name

Address

City   State/Province   Zip/Postal Code

Country

Tel   Fax

E-Mail

May we use your e-mail address for confirmations and other types of information? ❑ Yes ❑ No We appreciate receiving
your e-mail address. Haworth would like to e-mail special discount offers to you, as a preferred customer.
We will never share, rent, or exchange your e-mail address. We regard such actions as an invasion of your privacy.

Order from your **local bookstore** or directly from
The Haworth Press, Inc. 10 Alice Street, Binghamton, New York 13904-1580 • USA
Call our toll-free number (1-800-429-6784) / Outside US/Canada: (607) 722-5857
Fax: 1-800-895-0582 / Outside US/Canada: (607) 771-0012
E-mail your order to us: orders@haworthpress.com

For orders outside US and Canada, you may wish to order through your local
sales representative, distributor, or bookseller.
For information, see http://haworthpress.com/distributors

(Discounts are available for individual orders in US and Canada only, not booksellers/distributors.)

The Haworth Press, Inc.

Please photocopy this form for your personal use.
www.HaworthPress.com

BOF05